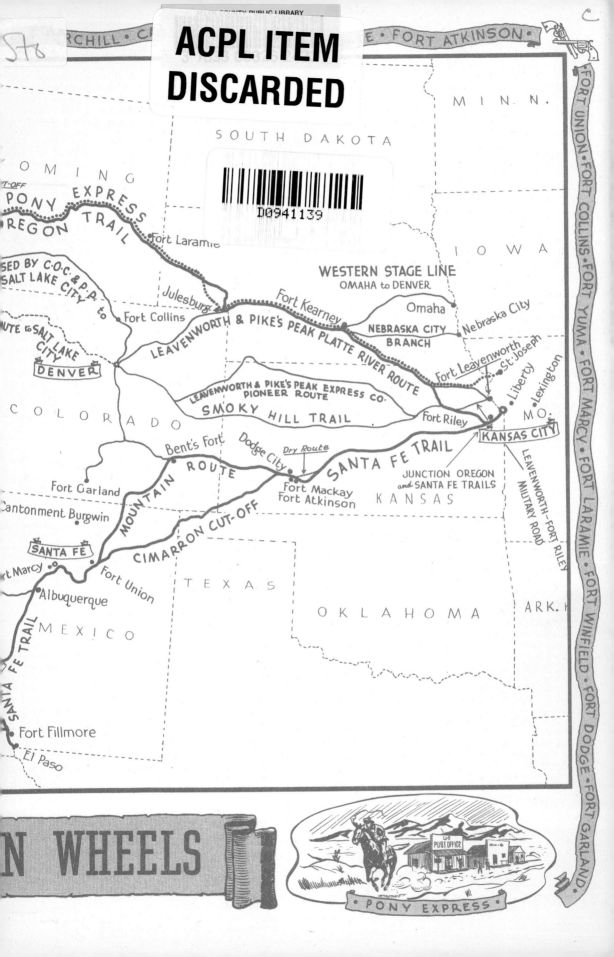

578

D0941139

MINN.

SOUTH DAKOTA

...T-OFF
PONY EXPRESS TRAIL
OREGON TRAIL
Fort Laramie

IOWA

SED BY C·O·C· & P·P·
SALT LAKE CITY to
...UTE to SALT LAKE CITY

WESTERN STAGE LINE
OMAHA to DENVER

Julesburg
Fort Collins
Fort Kearney
Omaha
Nebraska City
NEBRASKA CITY BRANCH
Nebraska City

LEAVENWORTH & PIKE'S PEAK PLATTE RIVER ROUTE

DENVER

Fort Leavenworth
St. Joseph
Lexington
Liberty

LEAVENWORTH & PIKE'S PEAK EXPRESS CO.
PIONEER ROUTE

SMOKY HILL TRAIL

COLORADO

Fort Riley

MO.

KANSAS CITY

Bent's Fort
Dodge City
Dry Route
SANTA FE TRAIL

MOUNTAIN ROUTE

Fort Garland

JUNCTION OREGON
and SANTA FE TRAILS

Cantonment Burgwin

Fort Mackay
Fort Atkinson

KANSAS

CIMARRON CUT-OFF

SANTA FE

...t Marcy
Fort Union

TEXAS

OKLAHOMA

ARK.

Albuquerque

MEXICO

SANTA FE TRAIL

Fort Fillmore

El Paso

N WHEELS

· PONY EXPRESS ·

U-S POST OFFICE

...RCHILL · C...
·E· FORT ATKINSON·

FORT UNION · FORT COLLINS · FORT YUMA · FORT MARCY · FORT LARAMIE · FORT WINFIELD · FORT DODGE · FORT GARLAND·

LEAVENWORTH-FORT RILEY MILITARY ROAD

EMPIRE ON WHEELS

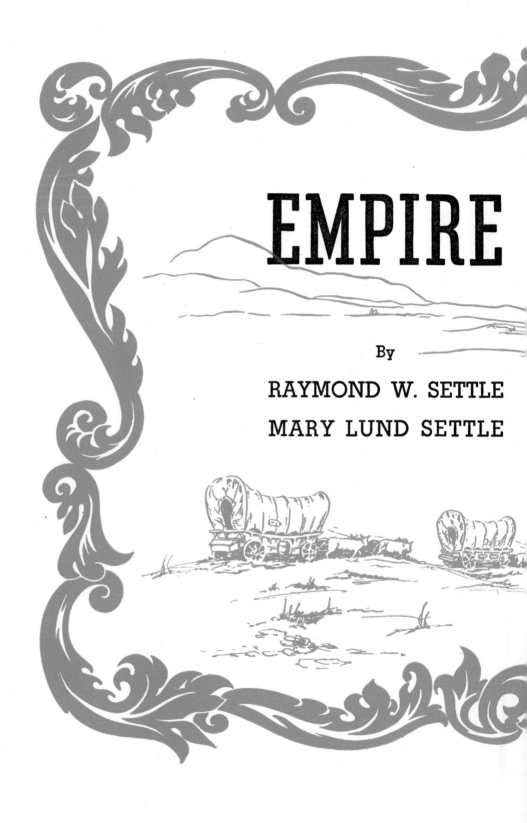

EMPIRE

By

RAYMOND W. SETTLE

MARY LUND SETTLE

ON WHEELS

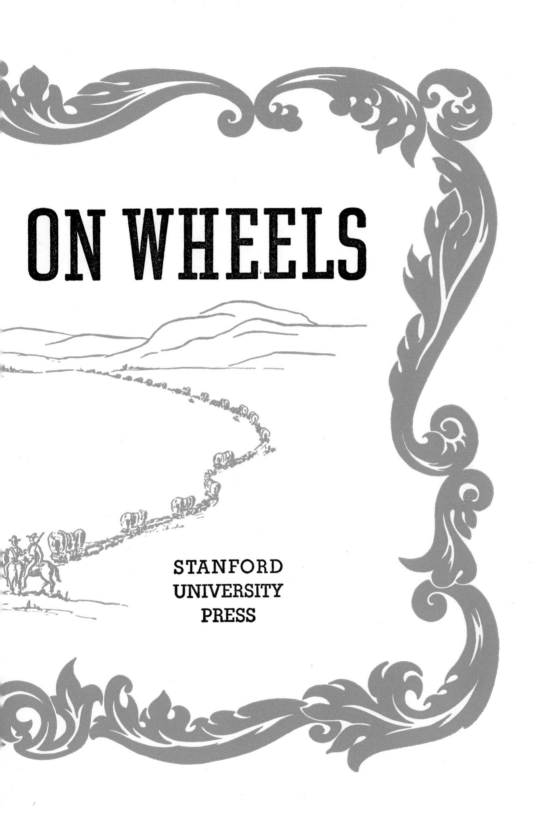

STANFORD
UNIVERSITY
PRESS

STANFORD UNIVERSITY PRESS, STANFORD, CALIFORNIA

THE BAKER AND TAYLOR COMPANY, 55 FIFTH AVE., NEW YORK 3, N. Y.
HENRY M. SNYDER & CO., 440 FOURTH AVE., NEW YORK 16, N. Y.
W. S. HALL & COMPANY, 457 MADISON AVE., NEW YORK 22, N. Y.

To Grandfather James F. Settle, who was
a bullwhacker for Alexander Majors, and
to Great-Grandfather Isham Majors, who
was a wagon master for Russell,
Majors & Waddell

FOREWORD

THE NAMES, Russell, Majors, and Waddell, call to mind mid-nineteenth-century, giant freighting operations on the Great Plains, stagecoach lines connecting Missouri River settlements with Salt Lake City, and galloping pony riders dispatching mails along the California Trail.

Basing their work upon much hitherto unused documentary material, Raymond W. Settle and Mary Lund Settle have in this book provided new interpretations of pre-railroad transportation in the Far West.

It is perhaps well for readers of *Empire on Wheels* to recall both the background and setting for this history. In what respects were the operations of Russell, Majors, and Waddell both like and unlike earlier American experiences in the field of transportation? What other methods and systems of transportation were in vogue in the East at the time when, with methods current in late Colonial times, the famed trio were helping to conquer the American Far West? And who, in the Far West, were the contemporaries of the Russell, Majors & Waddell company?

Unlike pioneers on the prairie and in the Great Basin region, people in Colonial times lived near the numerous rivers, inlets, and bays adjoining the Atlantic, and water provided the most suitable means of transportation and travel. Brigs, barks, schooners, and sloops carried men and cargoes across oceans and to neighboring coastal towns. Even farmers without direct access to seaports used water transportation—flatboats, "fall-boats," rafts, and other river craft—for moving their produce to market.

Vehicles were scarce articles during the first century of colonization. Nearly a century passed before private coaches appeared, and it was 1759 before commercial staging began in the form of springless Jersey wagon service between New York City and Philadelphia. And it was not until the middle of the eighteenth century that the Colonial West, namely the Pennsylvania Dutch, produced the famed Conestoga wagon with its sturdily built running gear and canvas-covered, boat-like body. It was the Conestoga which facilitated the extension of settlement into trans-Alleghenia; it was the descendant of this marvelous wagon, the prairie schooner, which made possible a hundred years ago the conquest of the American Far West and the building of an "Empire on Wheels."

The trans-Allegheny West (especially the lower Ohio and Mississippi regions) was, like the Atlantic seaboard, blessed with navigable streams. But to the distress of the commercial and manufacturing East, most of the goods produced in this new area first flowed south to New Orleans rather than east.

It was to combat the laws of gravity that, at the opening of the nineteenth century, an Eastern-dominated Congress provided funds for the construction of the National Road which began at Cumberland, Maryland, wound its way through the rugged Alleghenies to Wheeling on the Ohio River, on to Zanesville, Ohio, and then straight westward past Indianapolis to the Illinois boundary.

The National Road was a great boon to wagon transportation. Governmental postal contracts provided the impetus for extended stagecoach services into the Middle West, whereas the Great Migration to the Ohio Valley boomed the wagon freighting business.

By the time Missouri achieved statehood in 1821, steamboats, too, had arrived in the Middle West to challenge the more primitive rafts, flatboats, keelboats, and barges which until then had been the mainstay of Western river and lake transportation. It was in 1819 that the first steamer paddled up the Missouri as far as Council Bluffs; and a decade later regular packets operated between St. Louis on the east side of Missouri state and Fort Leavenworth on the west side.

As for canal construction, this would scarcely be called an innovation to most Americans of this particular period, and yet the construction of the Erie Canal (completed in 1825) far outstripped anything of its kind. The Erie Canal made possible the commercial ascendancy of New York City; it made possible, to a degree not achieved by the National Road, the drastic reduction of freight rates between the East and the Middle West. Many Western states were stimulated by the success of the Erie to build elaborate canal systems, but the coming of the railroad limited the usefulness of canals and in time largely displaced these man-made waterways.

It was in 1828 that the first groundwork of the Baltimore & Ohio, the earliest major railroad, was laid. Even though two decades elapsed before this line reached the Ohio River, there existed, in 1848, approximately one hundred small, scattered rail lines east of the Mississippi River.

Thus, at mid-century, by the time the United States stood at the crossroads of its western expansion, there had emerged (east of the Mississippi River) the variegated transportation systems to which references have been made. All systems known to modern civilization were in use; no one mode of travel or transport predominated. A person, who in 1848 may have traveled in the most direct manner from New York City to Independence, Missouri, would have utilized railroad, canalboat, ferryboat, steamboat, and stagecoach transport to reach his destination. When in 1845, for example, Nathaniel Fish Green, president of Columbia University, traveled from New York to St. Louis, he went by steamer up the Hudson River to Albany, by rail to Buffalo (he could, of course, have taken a canalboat on the Erie), by steamer to Detroit, by stagecoach to Galena, Illinois, and again by steamer to St. Louis. Returning, President Green traveled by steamer from St. Louis to Wheeling, by stagecoach to Cumberland, and by rail back home to New York City.

During this half-century an acquisitive American people had set its sights for the waters of the Pacific. The Louisiana Purchase extended the boundaries of the United States to the Rocky Mountains. Treaties with England opened the old Oregon country to joint occupancy and in 1846 brought about settlement of the Oregon boundary dispute. Then, following a long period of peaceful penetration, came the war with Mexico, followed in 1848 by the cession of California and the Great Southwest. Manifest Destiny had then reached floodtide, and with dramatic suddenness an American dream of empire had been realized.

No less breathtaking than political acquisition of the trans-Mississippi West is the story of its exploitation by means of trade and settlement. To be sure, this exploitation began early in the national period. Not long after independence, Yankee traders made the Pacific coast an important link in their Chinese trade. In the footsteps of Lewis and Clark, American fur traders first ventured up the Missouri and ultimately to the Columbia River Valley, southwest to Santa Fe, into the Great Basin, and finally across the Sierra Nevada into Mexican California. Mountain men often became permanent settlers in the Far West, as did missionaries.

In 1841 began the annual covered-wagon migrations to Oregon and

California, and by 1847 the Mormons had started their trek to the Great Salt Lake.

It is within the framework of the above-mentioned national developments in transportation that Raymond W. Settle and Mary Lund Settle have so ably written *Empire On Wheels*.

The curtain rises with "Wheels Rolling Toward Sunset," namely the Santa Fe Trail and the Santa Fe trade in which Russell participated. It was, however, not this Mexican trade but rather American military requirements—the Army's need for transport to its western bases—that gave impetus to the firm of Russell, Majors & Waddell. Supplying the Army of Utah at a time when a Mormon war was imminent is a subject thoroughly treated by the authors. Also handled with deftness are the many intricacies surrounding the Great Plains stagecoach and Pony Express businesses, which not only served interior communities (see the maps) but also linked rampaging California, as well as the bustling Middle West, with the railroading, steamboating East. In these enterprises the principals were deeply involved, and, for reasons made clear by the authors, the finale was inescapable ruin.

Access to previously unused source materials not only enabled the authors to present, as stated at the outset, a new interpretation of their subject, it made it possible for them to develop in greater detail certain phases heretofore treated but casually. Biographical information on Russell, Majors, and Waddell has been elaborated upon, and the distinctiveness of their respective personalities is made clear and understandable—a matter highly essential to an adequate understanding of the internal rifts among the company officers. For the first time a comprehensive view is given of how wagon trains were managed, how numerous they were, how valuable were their cargoes, how essential they were to military operations on the Plains, and how vital they were to westward migration and settlement.

In reading this book one should, of course, not be unmindful of events in Far Western transportation contemporary with the activities of Russell, Majors & Waddell. By 1855, in California, Wells, Fargo & Company became supreme among express companies, and between 1865 and the completion of the first transcontinental railroad this same company emerged as czar of western transportation. The same year, 1858, which found freighting on the Plains at a peak, also witnessed inauguration of the Butterfield Overland passenger and mail service along a 2,757-mile, deep-southern course from St. Louis to San Francisco. Similar services, successively represented by Ben Holladay and Wells, Fargo & Company—not to mention scores of minor entrepreneurs—followed in the wake of an ever-widening mineral frontier that engulfed Nevada, the Inland Empire, and still later, the Southwest.

Empire On Wheels contains a story sufficient unto itself. But it is also closely related to the other volumes in the Stanford University Press transportation series. It provides a much-needed part in a series which, though not originally conceived as a closely integrated set under single editorship, is seemingly evolving into a mosaic of early-day transportation in the trans-Mississippi West. In addition to filling an important niche in the Stanford University Press series, *Empire on Wheels* should become a friendly bookshelf companion of certain items not members of the Stanford family. *Empire On Wheels* is a logical preface to *Ben Holladay: The Stagecoach King* by J. V. Frederick; it is an important supplement to such other books as *The Overland Mail* by Leroy Hafen, and a companion piece to *Old Waybills* by Alvin Harlow, *The Pony Express* by Arthur Chapman, and *Six Horses* by William Banning and George H. Banning. They all help to make the old West live again as a vital part of American national experience.

OSCAR OSBURN WINTHER

INDIANA UNIVERSITY

PREFACE

THIS BOOK is the story of William H. Russell, Alexander Majors, and William Bradford Waddell. It describes the intricate ramifications of the firm they organized—the vast military freighting monopoly they exercised from 1855 to 1861, their far-flung stagecoach, express, and mail business (the origin of the famous Pony Express)—and their complex mercantile interests. To set down all this material, as one can readily see from reading the following pages, was an undertaking of almost forbidding proportions.

In all the history of the West there is no individual or group comparable to this colorful trio. Beginning life at the bottom of the ladder, they climbed to dizzy heights by sheer native ability, vision, and daring.

The pooling of the abilities and resources of these men in the firm of Majors & Russell enabled them to secure a monopoly on the business of freighting military supplies to the various army posts in the West and made necessary the creation of a working organization of incredible proportions. It also afforded them an opportunity to engage in the mercantile business, both as partners and as individuals, over an area bounded by the Missouri River on the east and by Salt Lake City, Denver, and Santa Fe on the west.

The first venture of any of the partners outside the freighting, mercantile, and banking business was in 1859, when Russell and John S. Jones organized the Leavenworth & Pike's Peak Express Company to run a line of Concord coaches from Leavenworth to Denver. When the stage line was transferred to the Platte River route and permanent stations established, each one became more or less of a trading point for travelers, emigrants, and settlers.

The organization of the Central Overland California & Pike's Peak Express Company in 1860 and the operation of the Pony Express were two of the most ambitious, romantic enterprises in the history of the nation. This corporation, which subsequently became the Overland Mail

Company and was later absorbed in Wells, Fargo & Company, constituted the link between the stagecoach and the railway express business. It was organized with an eye upon the latter and whoever owned it possessed a steppingstone toward the railway express contracts.

As frontier businessmen, Russell and Waddell, who were engaged in extensive merchandising at Lexington, Missouri, for more than twenty years before Majors opened his stores in Auraria and Kansas City, exercised far-reaching influence over the business and economic structure of western Missouri. Lexington, for approximately thirty years after its founding in 1822, was the most important retail and wholesale center in that part of the state. Wagons loaded with goods, which had been shipped up the Missouri River by steamboat, rolled out from there to points in southern and northern Missouri and to Sante Fe. Lexington also was the center for much of the fur trade of the distant Rocky Mountains.

From 1855 to 1861, Russell, Majors, and Waddell were regarded as the most influential, most substantial businessmen in the West. Their notes, acceptances, and drafts were readily negotiable anywhere and for any amount within the broad limits of reason. Their purchases of oxen, corn, hogs, and other farm products bolstered agriculture in western Missouri and Kansas Territory, and the wages paid their employees constituted a financial back-log for the same area.

Their contribution to the settlement of the Rocky Mountain region in the form of transportation, express and mail facilities, and the freighting of essential supplies was incalculable. They, more than any other individual or group, bridged the wide gap between the Missouri River and the broad West in those few important years between the Mexican War and the Civil War.

The fact that they suffered bankruptcy and that the limitless empire on wheels they built, at tremendous expenditure of energy and money, passed to the control of others, in no wise detracts from the credit due them. On the day they relinquished control of it, the chug of the steam locomotive and the click of the telegraph instrument were heard west of the Missouri River. Soon the gently swaying stagecoach, loaded with weary passengers, and the ponderous Conestogas, Pittsburgs, and Murphys, drawn by twelve to sixteen patient oxen, would disappear, but the names of these men, who generously contributed their treasure and the best years of their lives to keep them moving, will never be forgotten.

The authors' search for unknown and unused original source material concerning the careers of William H. Russell and William B. Waddell was greatly favored by five years' residence in Lexington, Missouri. During those years a quality and thoroughness of research in county records, old newspapers, and other sources, which would not have been possible under any other circumstances, was successfully carried on. The result was a gratifying mass of biographical data which accounts for the hitherto unknown years in the lives of these men.

The search also yielded a mass of letters, financial statements, contracts, and miscellaneous items, amounting in all to more than a thousand, from the private files of William B. Waddell. This valuable collection, loaned to us by Mrs. William B. Waddell of Lexington, is now owned by the Huntington Library, San Marino, California. Additional material of this nature was secured in California, Colorado, Kansas, Missouri, New York, Pennsylvania, Tennessee, and Washington, D.C. This project, which involved many thousands of miles of travel, was in part made possible by a grant-in-aid from the Huntington Library.

The authors are indebted to a host of friends who, in one manner or another, lent kindly assistance. To record all their names here would be impossible. The following, however, made such valuable contributions that to omit their names would be a sign of ingratitude. Special acknowledgments are due Mrs. Waddell for the loan of the Waddell Collection; Mr. B. M. Little and the Lexington Historical Society for the use of newspapers and the Aull Collection; Mrs. J. W. Russell, Mrs. R. G. Champion, William H. Russell; Mrs. Fanny Bane and Miss Sarah Russell for the use of photographs, family records, etc.; Miss Louisa P. Johnston for material and photographs relating to Alexander Majors; Miss Louise Kampf, Coburn Library, Colorado Springs, for the loan of books; Mr. Floyd C. Shoemaker, of the Missouri State Historical Society; Miss Stella Drumm, of the Missouri Historical Society; Dr. Leroy R. Hafen, of the Colorado State Historical Society; Mr. Kirke Mechem, of the Kansas State Historical Society; Mr. James C. Olsen, of the Nebraska State Historical Society; Mr. Elmer M. Hunt, of the New Hampshire State Historical Society; Mr. Leslie E. Bliss, Huntington Library; Miss Opal Carlin, Librarian, William Jewell College; Miss Elsie Evans, Leavenworth Public Library; Miss Julia T. Lynch, Salt Lake City Public Library; Miss Grace Berger, Kansas City (Mo.) Public Library; Mr. Paul North Rice, New York City Public Library; Mr. Arthur H. Cole, Librarian, Graduate School of Business Administration, Harvard University; Mr. Gerald J. Davis, National Archives, Washington, D.C.; Dr. Kate L. Gregg; and Miss Lydia Cooper, who assisted in the preparation of the manuscript.

RAYMOND W. SETTLE
MARY LUND SETTLE

CONTENTS

ILLUSTRATIONS

I

WHEELS ROLLING
TOWARD THE SUNSET

O N JANUARY 29, 1822, two weary, frost-bitten men, mounted upon footsore horses, rode into Franklin, Missouri. They brought a report which set the frontier buzzing with excitement, and which was to propel Manifest Destiny a long step farther westward. One of the men was Captain William Becknell, who eight months earlier had led a party of twenty to thirty men out into the silence and mystery of the Great American Desert, headed toward the legendary Rocky Mountains to trap and trade with the Indians.[1]

Their undertaking, so far as they had known when they started, was dangerous business. Under the Spanish rule, Americans were not welcome in New Mexico. To set foot south of the Arkansas River in those days was to invite imprisonment in a Mexican *calabozo*. Everybody on the frontier knew about Robert McKnight, who tried it in 1812, and had been kept within stone walls in the city of Chihuahua ever since.

Out upon the Plains somewhere or in the mountains, Captain Becknell probably received information from somebody that the picture had changed. Or, knowing that the Spaniards no longer ruled the country, he deliberately took the risk that it had and boldly entered forbidden territory. Again, he may have relied upon the ability of his twenty or thirty Missouri lads to shoot their way out of trouble if it developed.

Be all that as it may, about November 1, 1821, they met a squad of Mexican soldiers near San Miguel, New Mexico, who invited them to carry their goods on to Santa Fe. Accepting the invitation and leaving most of the party there, Captain Becknell rode on in, arriving on the 14th. What the soldiers had told him was true. Instead of being jailed, his brief stay in the old capital was delightfully pleasant. The Governor invited him to dine in the palace, asked him innumerable questions concerning the United States, expressed a desire that the Americans would

[1] Captain William Becknell, "Journal," pp. 78-80.

continue to bring goods to Santa Fe, and even suggested that immigrants would be welcome.

Scarcely believing his good fortune, Captain Becknell quickly sold his goods, packed the heavy silver dollars he received for them in rawhide bags, and returned to San Miguel. In late December, accompanied only by a man named McLaughlin, whose first name is not mentioned, Becknell set out on the nine-hundred-mile journey across the open, windswept plains back to Franklin. On this, the first recorded crossing of the Great American Desert in the middle of the winter, they probably followed what was later called the Cimarron Cutoff instead of attempting to negotiate the snow-clogged Raton Mountains. In forty-eight days they reached their destination. They had seen no hostile Indians, nobody had died on the way, hardships on the journey were not too great, the Mexicans were hungry for American goods, and the door to traffic with Santa Fe was at last open.

Captain Becknell exhibited his Mexican dollars and calmly announced plans to form another party and transport his goods to Santa Fe in wagons. Having traveled the long road twice, he was convinced it presented no obstacles to wheeled vehicles. Consequently, in May, 1822, he boldly pointed three ordinary, canvas-covered farm wagons toward the sunset and broke trail for the great caravans of prairie schooners, the steel rails and concrete highways yet to come.[2]

None of the twenty-one men accompanying the wagons realized the significance of their journey or knew that they were writing the beginning of a new, romantic chapter in American transportation. Moreover, the ultimate influence of the trade they were helping to inaugurate and the trail they were pioneering, upon the history of the nation and the westward march of empire, was wholly beyond anybody's comprehension at that time.

This journey was also successful. Since Captain Becknell makes no mention of the wagons being brought back, it may be assumed that they were sold to the Mexicans. The introduction of wheeled vehicles upon the great plains assured the inevitable march of the Americans to the far-off Pacific Ocean. Traders to Santa Fe and elsewhere could use pack horses if necessary. Home-seeking emigrants with their families had to negotiate those endless miles in wagons. Although it would be

[2] Becknell, "Journal of Two Expeditions from Boon's Lick to Santa Fe," pp. 57-65.

fourteen years before vehicles of this type would leave the Missouri River and head westward along the Oregon Trail, Captain Becknell had proved that such journeys were possible.

His little party, with its quota of trade goods stowed away in wagons, inaugurated the romantic era of the merchant freighter upon the Great Plains. Before it was terminated half a century later by the laying of steel rails, millions of dollars' worth of merchandise was transported annually from the Missouri River to all parts of the West, and as far as the Pacific Ocean. In behalf of these hardy, versatile men who risked fortune and endured unbelievable hardship on the long Santa Fe Trail, it should be noted that they were the ones who developed the technique of prairie travel. They learned how to organize wagon trains and handle them to best advantage upon the road. These men also adopted oxen in place of mules and horses, after oxen had been introduced by Major Bennett Riley in 1829,[3] and they developed the great prairie schooner.

The era of military freighting upon the Great Plains dawned in 1846 with the outbreak of the war with Mexico, when General S. W. Kearney's diminutive Army of the West straggled off across the prairie to capture Santa Fe. To send an expeditionary force of 1,701 officers and men into enemy territory about a thousand miles from its base of supplies at Fort Leavenworth was not as foolhardy as it might seem. The merchant freighters to Santa Fe, Chihuahua, and other points far in the interior of Mexico had already demonstrated that any amount of goods desired could be transported over the Santa Fe Trail.

In 1846 and 1847 the Army organized its own trains and hired civilian drivers or bullwhackers. Owing to ignorance of Army officers concerning the highly specialized business of freighting across the Great Plains, inefficiency of bullwhackers, and efficiency of raiding Indians, this plan proved a total failure in 1847. War Department officials in Washington wisely acknowledged the inability of the Army to transport its own supplies and instructed the quartermaster at Fort Leavenworth to make contracts with civilian freighters.

To James Brown, of Independence, Missouri, went the first contract, dated May 18, 1848, under which he agreed to deliver 200,000 pounds of supplies to Santa Fe for 11¾ cents per pound. Little is known concerning him except that he was an experienced freighter. He loaded

[3] Fred S. Perrine, "Military Escorts on the Santa Fe Trail," *New Mexico Historical Review*, III, 268.

his wagons at Fort Leavenworth, made the long haul down the trail, had no trouble with the Indians, and delivered the supplies in good condition. For this service he received $23,000. His work was so satisfactory that the civilian contract system was adopted as a permanent one.[4]

The Treaty of Guadalupe Hidalgo, which terminated hostilities with Mexico in 1848, did not usher in an era of tranquillity in the Southwest and upon the Great Plains. Instead, it reintroduced a type of grim, bloody conflict which for several generations had been subsiding elsewhere in the nation—Indian wars. By the annexation of New Mexico and the regions to the west as far as the Pacific Ocean, the United States shouldered the heavy responsibility for keeping in subjection the fierce tribes who inhabited these areas. This task involved the establishment of permanent military posts with year-round garrisons. By 1849 there were seven of these with troops totaling 987. Ten years later the number of posts had risen to sixteen. Every one, situated as they were in barren regions incapable of supporting them, had to be supplied with goods hauled in wagons from the Missouri River.[5]

Early in 1849 James Brown formed a partnership with William Hepburn Russell of Lexington, Missouri, to carry on the business of freighting military supplies across the Plains.[6] On April 30 they signed a contract under the name of Brown & Russell to transport supplies from Fort Leavenworth to Santa Fe for $9.98 per hundred pounds. Their bond of $150,000 was signed principally by residents of Lexington, Missouri, among whom were William Bradford Waddell, Robert B. Bradford, and J. W. Waddell. Another of the signers was John S. Jones of Pettis County, Missouri, who would soon become Russell's partner.

Russell was a lineal descendant of Lord William Russell, who was beheaded July 21, 1683, because of participation in a plot against the English Crown. Almost a hundred years later, three of his descendants, David, Stephen and Benjamin Russell, emigrated to America. Benjamin settled in Vermont, where he married Betsy Ann Eaton. They had eleven children, one of whom, William Eaton, married Betsy Ann Hepburn, descendant of the ancient Hepburn clan of Scotland, who did not live many years. Russell then married her sister Myrtilla, by whom he had a

---

[4] U.S. Senate, 31st Cong., 1st sess., Ex. Doc. 26, pp. 137, 742, 743. *St. Louis Era*, Dec. 4, 1847.
[5] Walker D. Wyman, "The Military Phase of Santa Fe Freighting," *Kansas Historical Quarterly*, I, 423.　　　　　　　　　　[6] Sen. 31st Cong., 1st sess., Ex. Doc. 26, p. 24.

daughter, Adala Elizabeth, and a son, William Hepburn, the latter born on January 31, 1812.[7]

Family tradition holds that William Eaton Russell was a colonel in the War of 1812 and commanded the land forces in the little battle of Lake Champlain. He died in 1814 while still in the service, and his body was taken home to Burlington, Vermont, for burial. Among the officers in the funeral cortege was Second Lieutenant Oliver Bangs of the Third United States Artillery.[8] His acquaintance with Mrs. Russell ripened into love and they were married at Vergennes, Vermont, January 1, 1816.[9] On June 1, 1821, Lieutenant Bangs was honorably discharged from the United States Army with the rank of first lieutenant. A few years later they emigrated to Western Missouri.

In 1828, at sixteen years of age, William H. Russell went to work as a clerk in the Ely & Curtis store in Liberty.[10] On January 1, 1829, Robert Aull and Samuel Ringo opened a store there. Aull was one of the noted trinity of brothers, John and James being the others, who, as Missouri's frontier chain-store operators, exercised a broad influence upon the Santa Fe trade, the fur trade, and the economic life of the West from the middle 1820's to the late 1840's. They established a store in Lexington in 1825, one in Independence in 1827, and another in Richmond in 1830. In the early part of the latter year, Russell was working for them at either Richmond or Lexington.[11]

Russell's formal education, whatever it may have been, ended when he went to work for Ely & Curtis in Liberty. He wrote a fair hand, which in later life degenerated into an almost indecipherable scrawl, used passably good grammar, and exhibited a flair for accounting.

The Missouri frontier, to which Russell came as a boy in the late 1820's, was the farthest limit of American civilization. Beyond it stretched the Great Plains, still regarded as the Great American Desert. The Missouri River, whose tawny waters churned restlessly down from the almost unknown Northwest, flowed past his doorstep. On its south bank, a few miles away, lay the Santa Fe Trail. Thus situated, he was, from the earli-

[7] William H. Russell, Letter (n.d.). Russell Family History (MS). *Dictionary of American Biography*, XVI, 252.

[8] Russell Family History. Heitman, *Historical Register*, I, p. 105.

[9] *Marriage Record*, Vergennes, Vermont, 1816.

[10] Russell Family History. *History of Clay and Platte Counties*, (Mo.), p. 100.

[11] James and Robert Aull, *Letter Book*, II, 1, 2, 5, 9, 14, 18, 135, 201.

est days of his business career, in intimate contact with both the Santa Fe trade and the fur trade of the Rocky Mountains. In the light of his later career this was highly significant.

In many respects the young Yankee from Vermont was wholly out of place on the raw, boisterous frontier. Although it was his home for over thirty years, he never loved it. An aristocrat by nature, he never took on a single characteristic of the frontiersman. He never wore buckskin or homespun, his clothes were always carefully tailored, he never "roughed it," never hunted or fished, never drove an ox team, and avoided sweat, hardship, and toil with his hands.

On June 9, 1835, he married Harriet Elliot, daughter of the Reverend John Warder, a Baptist minister whose home was near Lexington.[12] In March 1836, his eldest son John Warder was born. His first business venture was in 1837 when he helped organize the Lexington First Addition Company, subscribing for five of the eighty-seven shares.[13]

The following year he resigned his position with the Aulls to form a partnership with James S. Allen and William Early to open a retail store under the name of Allen, Russell & Company.[14] In 1840 he succeeded his old employer, James Aull, as treasurer of Lafayette County, which office he filled until 1855.[15] He was appointed postmaster at Lexington in 1841 and served four years.[16]

In the late 1830's and early 1840's, Lexington, being the fourth largest town in the state and the largest on the Western border, presented challenging business possibilities Russell could not resist. He formed a partnership with James H. Bullard and Dewitt J. Pritchard to open another store under the name of Bullard & Russell and became a partner in the firm of Waddell, Ramsay & Company whose business was the manufacture of hemp rope and bagging. Unfortunately the firm of Allen, Russell & Company failed in 1845. This was his first experience in bankruptcy but by no means his last.[17]

In spite of this one failure, the late 1840's were prosperous ones for Russell. He bought additional shares in the Lexington First Addition

---

[12] *Marriage Record Book* B, Lafayette County, Mo., p. 25.

[13] *Record Book* F, Lafayette County, Mo.

[14] *Lexington Express*, Feb. 24, 1842. *Record Book* F, Lafayette County, Mo., p. 510.

[15] James and Robert Aull, *Receipt Book*, V, 836-847.

[16] J. M. Donaldson to the author, Aug. 23, 1945.

[17] *Lexington Advertiser*, Oct. 13, 1845. *Record Book* I, Lafayette County, Mo., pp. 17, 387.

Company until he owned a controlling interest in it. In the meantime he bought some sixty town lots, upon one of which he built a twenty-room mansion, and about three thousand acres of Lafayette and Ray County land from the United States government.[18]

The year 1847 marked Russell's beginning as a freighter upon the Great Plains. That year his firm of Bullard & Russell joined with E. C. McCarty of Westport in loading out the first merchant train of private goods ever to leave Westport Landing, site of the future Kansas City, for Santa Fe. They sent another in 1848. A partnership with James Brown being formed in 1849 to transport military supplies, Russell temporarily withdrew from merchant freighting.[19]

In the spring of 1850, contracts for this work were let to the lowest bidder. Russell did not participate, but Brown and John S. Jones got one to deliver supplies to Fort Hall on the Snake River. In the latter part of the summer, possibly because of Indian raids, an extraordinary necessity for sending supplies to Santa Fe arose. Although the additional risk due to lateness in starting was great, Russell, Brown, and John S. Jones formed a partnership called Brown, Russell & Company, and on September 4 contracted to deliver 600,000 pounds of supplies in Santa Fe for 14 1/3 cents per pound. Robert Aull was interested in this business as a silent partner.[20]

Four trains of thirty wagons each and one of fifteen left Fort Leavenworth between September 14 and October 4. On the road they were organized into two caravans, with Brown himself in charge of one and Charles O. Jones, brother of John S., as assistant. This train arrived at the old Pecos River pueblo, some forty-five or fifty miles from Santa Fe, in the last half of November. Here they were snowbound by a sudden mountain blizzard. Leaving the caravan in camp, Brown rode on into Santa Fe to report the condition of things to the commandant of the garrison and gain permission to lay over until better weather prevailed. Immediately after his arrival he became ill with typhoid fever and erysipelas, and he died on December 5.[21]

---

[18] *Record Books* F to M, Lafayette County, Mo. *Book of Original Entries*, Lafayette County, Mo. Aull, *Letter Book* IV, 334; *Lexington Express*, March 25, 1845.

[19] Theo. S. Case, *History of Kansas City.* p. 33. U.S. Senate, 31st Cong., 2d sess., Ex. Doc. 11, p. 15.

[20] Sen., 31st Cong., 1st sess., Ex. Doc. 1, p. 295.

[21] Sen., 36th Cong., 2d sess., Report of Committee on Military Affairs, p. 311; Aull, *Letter Book* IV, 270, 273, 275, 283, 286, 289, 307, 308, 313, 316, 317, 336, 444, 452, 465, 518, 529, 539.

After waiting several days for Brown's return, Jones also went on to Santa Fe. His request for delay in taking the road was refused and an ultimatum delivered that unless the train moved immediately the army would bring it in at the contractor's expense. There being no alternative, Jones returned to camp to do his best. He got the wagons to Santa Fe but had to spend some $14,000 for forage and new oxen to replace those which died under the yoke. Russell prepared a memorial to Congress asking for $39,800 on account of losses incurred by this train. The other one followed the Arkansas River to Bent's Fort, where it remained until spring.

The surviving partners carried on in 1851 as Jones & Russell. On February 17 they contracted to deliver an unspecified amount of supplies to Santa Fe and Albuquerque for $8.50 and $9.50 per one hundred pounds, respectively, during that and the following year. This was the first instance where a two-year contract was given. In May they signed another to deliver supplies at Las Vegas, Mora, and Rayado for $7.87 per one hundred pounds. In addition they contracted to deliver twelve thousand bushels of corn at Fort Kearny for $2.07 per bushel.[22] Robert Aull was again interested in the business. When this contract was concluded Jones temporarily passed from the scene as Russell's partner.

Freighting military supplies for the government was profitable and Russell's interests continually expanded. In 1850 he helped organize the Lexington Mutual Fire and Marine Insurance Company and was elected president in 1854. He helped organize Lexington Female Collegiate Institute in 1851. Early in 1855, when it was reorganized as Lexington Baptist Female College, he was the heaviest subscriber. In 1851 he became a member of the merchandising firm of Morehead, Waddell & Company. About a year later he and William B. Waddell bought Morehead's interest and changed the name to Waddell & Russell. This firm became a part of the great concern of Majors & Russell in 1855 and of Russell, Majors & Waddell in 1858.[23]

[22] Sen., 32d Cong., 1st sess., Ex. Doc. 1, p. 295. Aull, *Letter Book* V, 246.

[23] William Young, *History of Lafayette County, Mo.*, I, 212. *Lexington Weekly Express*, Jan. 12, 1852, Sept. 10, 1859. Minutes, Board of Trustees, Lexington Baptist Female College, June 15, 1855.

II

THE FREIGHTING MONOPOLY

THE IMMIGRANT ANCESTOR of the American Waddells was John, who was born in Glasgow, Scotland, in 1724. At eleven years of age he was brought to America by a man named Carter, to whom he was apprenticed. They settled in Fauquier County, Virginia, where young Waddell grew to manhood. In 1757 he married Elizabeth Green. His seventh child, also named John, married Catherine Bradford, a descendant of Governor William Bradford of Plymouth Colony. Their eldest son, William Bradford, was born October 17, 1807. Four years later the mother died, the father married Sarah Crow in 1813, and the family migrated to Mason County, Kentucky, in 1815.[24]

Living as he did upon the highroad to the newest Land of Promise beyond the Mississippi, it was inevitable that the impulse to join the procession of emigrants should seize William Bradford Waddell. In 1824 he went to Galena, Illinois, where he worked in the newly opened lead mines. After a brief stay there he went to St. Louis, where he clerked in the store of Berthoud & McCreery. Here at the back door of the East and the front door of the West, he heard much to interest him. The fur trade was beginning to boom and people talked big about the possibilities of the new Santa Fe trade. There was also much talk about the Boon's Lick country and the new towns of Lexington and Liberty, up on the western border of Missouri. He never forgot these things.

When he grew tired of clerking in a store in St. Louis he returned to Mason County with his memories and information. He got another job as clerk in a store in Washington, Kentucky, but this did not last long. Then his father put him upon a farm. This proved to be a fortunate move, for near by lived charming Susan Byram. After a brief courtship they were married January 1, 1829. With typical Southern gen-

24 Mrs. Alonzo Slayback, "Genealogy of the John Waddell Family," MS. Paul I. Wellman, "The Silent Partner," *Kansas City Star,* Nov. 22, 1942. Aull, *Order Book* V, 329. *Lexington Weekly Express,* July 4, 1840. Minutes, First Baptist Church, Lexington, Mo., May 20, 1840.

erosity the bride's father gave them Negroes, horses, sheep, fifteen hundred dollars in cash, and a big, fat feather bed. But farming was not the answer to what was germinating in the young husband's soul. Some years later he moved to Mayslick, Kentucky, where he opened a dry-goods store.

The business prospered, but it was not the answer either. The trans-Mississippi country was always in his mind. In 1835 or early in 1836, he sold his business and moved to Lexington, Missouri. He built a store on the river front near Jack's Ferry and stocked it with goods, some of which he bought from the Aull brothers. Although only twenty-nine years of age he was immediately recognized as a man of more than ordinary ability. Having become a Baptist in Kentucky, he united with the Reverend Warder's church, of which Russell also became a member.

Waddell prospered in Lexington. He operated both a wholesale and retail business and dealt in produce, hemp, and grain. Like Russell, he also bought several thousand acres of government land. He was a shareholder in the Lexington First Addition Company, and he helped organize the Lexington Mutual Fire and Marine Insurance Company and the Lexington Female Collegiate Institute. When it was reorganized as the Lexington Baptist Female College, he became one of the trustees. In 1851 he became a member of the firm of Morehead, Waddell & Company, which about a year later became Waddell & Russell.

Although two men could scarcely have been more unlike than Russell and Waddell, they were irresistibly drawn together from the day they met. Russell's traditions and antecedents ran back through Vermont to Merrie England, Waddell's through Virginia to foggy, chilly Scotland. Both erected mansions on South Street, just across the way from each other, and each kept open house in true Southern style.

In 1848 Robert Aull remarked, concerning a business proposition, that "Russell is generally too sanguine." [25] That observation by a wise contemporary who had known him intimately for many years serves as a key to an understanding of Russell's whole business career. The source of that sanguinity, which at times drove him to sheer recklessness, was a perfect, unwavering confidence in his own judgment and ability.

Waddell was the opposite of all this. Although generally animated by hopeful confidence, his disposition was certainly not sanguine. His

[25] *Letter Book* V, 138.

decisions were the result of ponderous deliberation. He also believed in his own judgment and ability, but that faith was haltered by cool, calculating reason.

Russell was volatile, highly temperamental, and a bundle of supercharged nerves. Waddell was phlegmatic, stolid, and inclined to sulk when crossed. They quarreled again and again, yet were always loyal to each other. At times Waddell's better judgment prompted him to break away from his impetuous partner, but he was never able to do so.

In 1853 Waddell & Russell contracted to deliver military supplies at Fort Riley for $7.00 per hundred pounds and at Fort Union for $16.00. When the season closed the company had made a good profit although it had put only two or three trains upon the road.[26]

When the successful bidders for contracts in 1854 were announced, Waddell & Russell was not among them. Not finding a suitable market for its outfit, the company parked most of the wagons, loaded one train with trade goods and sent it to California in charge of R. W. Durham. Along with it went the firm's surplus oxen. The train arrived in the vicinity of Sacramento September 8, having lost one man and twenty percent of the animals on the road.[27]

After the war with Mexico, agitation for railroads west of the Mississippi and to California was stepped up. Out in western Missouri the people began holding county conventions to consider the question of rails. Instead of soaring off into panegyrics concerning a road to the Pacific Ocean, they debated the more modest plan of linking county seats and other towns. Russell and other Lexingtonians took a deep interest in the matter. He helped organize the Lexington & Boonville Railroad Company in 1853, the Lexington & Davies County Railroad in 1854, and was a member of the Board of Directors of both.[28]

While the Waddell & Russell wagon train and herd of oxen were crawling across the Plains toward California in the fall of 1854, the partners were busy with a new idea—freighting military supplies across the Plains. The plan was nothing less than to form a partnership with Alexander Majors of Westport, Missouri, and to secure a monopoly on the

---

[26] U.S. House of Rep., 33d Cong., 1st sess., Ex. Doc. 63, pp. 33, 34.

[27] Sen., 33d Cong., 2d sess., Ex. Doc. 68. *Lexington Weekly Express,* April 26, May 31, Nov. 8, 1854. Russell to Waddell, Oct. 25, 1858.

[28] *Lexington Weekly Express,* Oct. 20, 22, 1852.

business. As a result, the three men signed a two-year agreement, dated December 28, 1854, to become effective January 1, 1855.[29]

This agreement provided that they should engage "in the buying and selling of goods wares and merchandize and also in a general trading in stock waggons teams and other things used in the outfitting of persons teams or trains across the plains or elsewhere and also in freighting goods or freight for Government or others . . . ." The business was to be conducted in Lexington under the name of Waddell, Russell & Company, and in Jackson County under Majors & Russell. The capital stock was fixed at $60,000, one-third of which was furnished by each. The physical assets of the new firm were very large. It took over the Waddell & Russell store in Lexington and had branch produce houses at Dover, Berlin, Wellington, and Sibley. It probably also had a branch of some kind in Independence.

Majors was born near Franklin County, Kentucky, October 4, 1814.[30] In 1818 his father, Benjamin, loaded the family into a covered wagon and set out for Missouri. They spent the following winter near the present site of Glasgow and located in the neighborhood of Fort Osage, in Jackson County, early in 1819. On November 6, 1834, Alexander was married to Miss Catherine Stalcup of that county,[31] having in the meantime begun farming operations of his own. They moved to Cass County, Missouri, where they settled upon a farm near the headwaters of Grand River.

In spite of the fact that he was successful in a modest way, there was an increasing sense of uneasiness in his heart. Most of his growing family were girls and the question of whether he would be able singlehanded to feed, clothe, and properly educate them became more insistent. By 1846 he knew he had to do something different; consequently, that summer he loaded a wagon with goods and drove up the Kaw River to the Pottawatomie Indian Reservation on a trading expedition.[32]

This expedition, aside from its financial angles, was important for it set Majors to thinking about taking to the plains as a freighter. "I was brought up to handle animals," he said about half a century later, "and had been employed more or less in the teaming business. After

[29] Contract between William H. Russell, Alexander Majors, and William B. Waddell, Dec. 28, 1854.

[30] Alexander Majors, *Seventy Years on the Frontier*, p. 15.

[31] *Marriage Record* No. 1, Jackson County, Mo., p. 75.

[32] *Kansas City Star*, Jan. 15, 1900, Jan. 29, 1927.

WILLIAM H. RUSSELL

ALEXANDER MAJORS

WILLIAM B. WADDELL

JOHN W. RUSSELL

looking the situation all over it occurred to me there was nothing I was so well adapted for by my past experience as the freighting business that was then being conducted between Independence, Mo., and Santa Fe, New Mexico." [33]

In 1848 he bought six wagons, a sufficient number of oxen to draw them, wrote out a pledge for his bullwhackers to sign,[34] and became a working member of a hard, weatherbeaten fraternity whose like will never be seen again. This much discussed and frequently ridiculed pledge was a matter of everyday common sense, with a considerable element of sincere religious sentiment thrown in. He believed that orderly, sober, God-fearing men made the most efficient employees and would tolerate no other kind. Not all bullwhackers were ruffians, rowdies, or moral degenerates. Some were, it is true, but they did not work for Alexander Majors. Many of them were respectable, serious-minded family men, who happened to follow that vocation as an honorable means of livelihood. Another thing he insisted upon was lying in camp and resting on the Sabbath day.

From whom Majors got his first contract to Santa Fe in 1848 or what he took out is not known. The cargo could have been his own but it was more likely that of someone else. Although the time for starting was late, he loaded his wagons at either Westport or Independence and set out on August 10. He got back November 2, having made the round trip in ninety-two days, the quickest on record.[35]

In 1849 he again made the trip, and by 1850 the business required 10 wagons and 130 oxen. His earnings for this year were $13,000. Immediately after his return home late in the summer, he heard that the quartermaster at Fort Leavenworth wished to send twenty wagonloads of supplies to Fort McKay, near the present Dodge City, Kansas. Although the usual time for starting was long since past, he contracted to transport 103,644 pounds for $7.00 per hundred. This was his first experience in the freighting of military supplies. The outbound trip was uneventful and he arrived on schedule with the supplies in good condition.

[33] Majors, *op. cit.*, p. 71.

[34] "While I am in the employ of A. Majors, I agree not to use profane language, not to get drunk, not to gamble, not to treat animals cruelly, and not to do anything else that is incompatible with the conduct of a gentleman. And I agree, if I violate any of the above conditions, to accept my discharge without any pay for my services." *Ibid.*, p. 72.

[35] *Ibid.*, p. 140.

Since the fort was under construction and the commandant's facilities for bringing logs from a creek some twenty-five miles away were limited, Majors next hired out his wagons and men for that purpose.[36]

He was on the trail to Santa Fe again with twenty-five wagons in 1851. For some reason he parked his wagons, sold his oxen to California emigrants, and remained at home in 1852. The following year he again outfitted himself and freighted private goods to Santa Fe. This year he again returned home in time for a second trip to Fort Union in the fall, hauling military supplies at $16 per hundred pounds. From 1853 on he was continually, though not exclusively, engaged in freighting for the government. The contract awarded him for transporting military supplies in 1854 required 100 wagons, 1,200 oxen, and about 120 men.[37] This was an excellent showing for a man who eight years earlier had driven one wagon up the Kaw River to trade with the Pottawatomie Indians. Well indeed would it have been for him had he been content with things as they were. Although he was prospering, he hazarded everything in an attempt to do better by forming the partnership with Russell and Waddell.

The two-year contract with the government, signed on March 27, 1855, under the name of Majors & Russell, gave these men a monopoly on transporting all military supplies west of the Missouri River. A new method of figuring rates, a fixed sum per one hundred pounds per one hundred miles, was employed. The schedule was:

To Fort Union and intermediate points $1.14 to $2.20; from that place to any other point in New Mexico $1.40 to $1.80.

To Salt Lake City and intermediate points $1.30 to $2.15.[38]

These rates applied only to loadings in April and May. Those made at later dates would come higher.

Leavenworth, Kansas, at that time a squatter town on the Delaware Indian Reservation two miles south of the fort, was chosen as headquarters for the firm. They built offices, warehouses, a blacksmith and wagon shop, and opened a store. The advertisement announcing its opening bore both the names of Majors, Russell & Company and Russell, Majors & Waddell. Charles R. Morehead Jr., Russell's nephew, was in charge of

36 Majors, *op cit.,* pp. 128, 137, 139. Sen., 32d Cong., 1st sess., Ex. Doc. 1, p. 295.
37 Majors, p. 140. H. R., 33d Cong., 1st sess., Ex. Doc. 17, p. 9.
38 H. R., 34th Cong., 1st sess., Ex. Doc. 17, p. 9.

it and his son John W. was bookkeeper. Within the next nine months the firm spent $15,000 for buildings and improvements. They opened a lumber yard and a packing plant to supply meat for their trains, and built a sawmill on Shawnee Creek ten miles to the south.[39]

When the last employee was hired the company roster bore the names of 1,700 employees. Twenty-five or thirty of these were wagon masters, a like number were assistants, forty or fifty were stock tenders, and twenty to thirty were cooks. Among the messengers employed to ride back and forth between trains on the road was ten-year-old William F. Cody, later known to world-wide fame as "Buffalo Bill." As soon as the contract was signed, the company sent out cattle buyers to comb the country for oxen. When they were through, the firm owned 7,500. The company began loading early in May, and when the last wagon rolled out upon the prairie, they had five hundred, a total of twenty trains, on the road.[40]

Each train of twenty-six wagons represented an investment of from $18,000 to $20,000.[41] The five hundred vehicles used in 1855 represented an investment of from $360,000 to $400,000. It is not at all probable that the partners had anything like that amount of capital at their disposal. With a contract, with experience and a reputation such as theirs, financing the company was a simple matter. Drafts payable in three to nine months were acceptable to anybody, and loans of cash were easily obtained. They went heavily into debt to promote the business in 1855. Owing to a series of unforeseeable misfortunes, they were never able to get out again.

In 1855, Kansas Territory was the focal point of national interest. Concern for its affairs had been kindled to white heat by the long, bitter debates in Congress over the Kansas-Nebraska Bill, immigration to it was strong, towns were being founded almost every day, agriculture was off to a good start, and every known type of business was springing up. All of this meant unprecedented opportunity.

With Majors to superintend the hiring of bullwhackers, loading the wagons, and getting them started on their long journey, Russell got busy

[39] Charles R. Morehead Jr., "Personal Recollections," in Connelley, *Doniphan's Expedition,* p. 602. A. O. Bangs to Waddell. Feb. 9, 1859. Contract between William H. Russell, Alexander Majors, and William B. Waddell, Dec. 28, 1854. *Leavenworth Herald,* Dec. 1, 1855.

[40] *Leavenworth Herald,* May 1, Dec. 3, 1855.

[41] Major & Russell, *Account of Losses,* Feb. 1860.

organizing subsidiary partnerships for the firm and developing interests of his own. Each of the partners invested heavily in Leavenworth real estate. Russell helped organize the town companies of Tecumseh, Louisiana, and Rochester. Majors found time to help promote the town of Wewoka. Russell organized the Leavenworth Fire and Marine Insurance Company and assisted in promoting the Leavenworth, Pawnee & Western Railroad. In the fall of 1855 he formed a partnership with Luther R. Smoot of Washington, D.C., to open a bank under the name of Smoot, Russell & Company.[42]

When the empty wagons arrived back at Leavenworth in the fall, they were turned over to wheelwrights, blacksmiths, and carpenters, to be gotten ready for the next year. The oxen were driven to various places to be wintered, the broken down ones were sold and new ones bought. Majors said that the company's profit for that year was about $150,000.

Early in 1856 a group of Lexingtonians, one of whom was Russell, built a large side-wheel steamboat which they christened the *William H. Russell*.[43] In the fall of that year the partners bought some ten thousand acres of Kansas farm lands for which they paid $83,721. Their profits on the freighting business for this year again amounted to about $150,000. The year 1856 marked the high tide in their fortunes. At that time they were richer than they ever had been or would be again. Majors said that they had from 300 to 350 wagons in service that year.

[42] James C. Horton, "Personal Narrative," *Kansas Historical Collections*, X, 597, and note; George W. Martin, "A Chapter from the Archives," *ibid.*, XII, 364. Paul W. Gates, "A Fragment of Kansas Land History," *Kansas Historical Quarterly*, VI, 234.

[43] *Lexington American Citizen*, June 23, 1856.

III

SUPPLYING THE ARMY OF UTAH

O N FEBRUARY 25, 1857, the partners signed a one-year contract, under the name of Majors & Russell, which renewed their monopoly on the transportation of not less than fifty thousand nor more than five million pounds of military supplies to posts in the West and Southwest.[44] It provided that notice of desired loadings should be given, the length of time varying with the number of pounds to be hauled, and it set up a schedule of pay similar to that of the previous contract. As usual their trains were upon the road by the middle of May.

Under ordinary circumstances, affairs would have proceeded as smoothly this year as they did in 1856 and 1857. Trouble with the Mormons in Utah, which had been in the making for some years, caused the administration to order United States troops to the scene of discord. On May 28, 1857, a small army, consisting of about twenty-five hundred men of the 5th and 10th Infantry under Colonel E. B. Alexander, the 2d Dragoons under Colonel Philip St. George Cooke and a battery of the 4th Artillery under Captain J. W. Phelps, was ordered to assemble at Fort Leavenworth to march to Utah with the old Indian fighter, General S. W. Harney, in command.

On June 19, Captain Thomas L. Brent, quartermaster at Fort Leavenworth, called upon Russell and served notice that the firm would be required to transport three million pounds of supplies to Utah in addition to what had already been sent elsewhere.[45] Russell's reply was that their trains were already upon the road, the time for getting ready was too short, and that to comply with the request would ruin Majors & Russell. Captain Brent admitted the truth of what Russell said but urged him to undertake the task anyway. The War Department, he said, depended upon Majors & Russell to perform this service. If they refused,

---

[44] Contract of Majors & Russell with Captain Thomas L. Brent, Feb. 16, 1857. Majors & Russell, *A Brief Statement of Claim. . . . ,* p. 26. Hereafter cited as *A Brief Statement.*

[45] Russell, "Statement," April 4, 1861. Majors & Russell, *A Brief Statement,* pp. 2, 32, 36-38.

there was grave doubt about the success of the whole enterprise. He also stated that he did not believe the government would allow the contractors to suffer loss because of it. Russell at length agreed, with the understanding that Captain Brent would assist him in making up and presenting a claim to Congress for additional remuneration. He afterward said that President Buchanan's cabinet assured Quartermaster General Thomas S. Jesup that the contractors would not be neglected.

What Majors & Russell should have demanded, and got, was a new contract covering the circumstances. In this vitally important matter both Russell and the War Department were at fault. In a claim later presented to Congress for losses and additional remuneration, Russell showed that whereas they received $14.27 per one hundred pounds per one hundred miles on the Utah supplies, they should have been paid in excess of $20.00. Failure to write a new contract was a grave mistake. In fact it was the beginning of a series of mistakes which brought ruin upon the firm.

Having agreed to transport the supplies, Majors & Russell quickly swung into action. John M. Dawson, John T. Bartleson, H. T. Chiles, and other veteran cattle buyers were sent out to bring in oxen at whatever price they could. Before the first day was over they discovered that an advance of 25 percent over ordinary prices was the rule. Bullwhackers asked a 50 percent increase in wages and the price of wagons was hiked. Russell said that all these things had such an unfavorable effect upon the firm's financial status that its credit was seriously impaired.

The Army of Utah got off from Fort Leavenworth between the middle of July and the first of August. A claim presented to Congress in 1860 shows that forty-one Majors & Russell trains carrying 4,525,913 pounds of supplies were billed for Utah. A contract to supply two thousand head of beef cattle was given the partners under the name of Waddell & Russell. For that year they had a total of fifty-nine trains upon the road to New Mexico, Utah, and elsewhere. This is almost half the number given by Russell in New York in 1861, but it is probably correct.[46]

A special road organization for handling the business was set up. James Rupe[47] was appointed general agent with Charles R. Morehead Jr.

[46] Nebraska State Historical *Publications*, XX, 390. Majors & Russell, *A Brief Statement*, p. 34.
[47] *A Brief Statement*, p. 34.

as assistant. This office was one of great responsibility and authority. They were empowered to receive and pay out money, buy forage, supplies, oxen, or anything else required to keep the wheels rolling. When the cargoes were delivered they could sell wagons, oxen, or equipment if necessary.

In addition to the general agent and his assistant, who moved from place to place, an agent was stationed at Fort Laramie. He was authorized to receive notice of supplies to be delivered, give receipts for goods, collect money due the firm, forward receipted bills of lading showing trains had passed that point, attend to other details relating to the business, draw drafts upon the firm and pay out money.

The trains made good time and reached Fort Laramie late in July. Eighteen which were billed through to Utah rolled on, reaching South Pass the latter part of August with Trains 1 and 2 in the advance. Here James Rupe received orders from Captain Stewart Van Vliet to halt all trains in the vicinity of Green River. Trains 1, 2, 3, and 4 went on, crossed Green River and halted on Ham's Fork about fifteen miles above its junction with Black's Fork. The advance guard of the army under Colonel E. B. Alexander was in camp here; the place was called Camp Winfield.[48]

When word that the army was on its way to Salt Lake City reached Governor Brigham Young he declared that the Mormons would burn and destroy everything in Salt Lake Valley if the soldiers set foot in it.[49] On September 15, he issued a proclamation declaring martial law in the Territory, forbade United States troops to enter it, and ordered the militia, numbering four or five thousand men, to be ready to march at a moment's notice. On October 4, General Daniel H. Wells ordered his men to stampede animals, burn trains, block roads with trees, destroy fords, and burn all grass. At the same time he ordered them to take no lives.

A number of parties, among which was one led by Major Lot Smith, rode out to obey these orders. On the night of October 4, they came upon Majors & Russell's Trains 21 and 25 in charge of Wagonmasters John M. Dawson and R. W. Barrett at a place called Simpson's Hollow on Green River. Train 26, in charge of Wagonmaster Lewis Simpson, was camped on Big Sandy Creek some fifteen miles to the rear. About midnight Smith's Mormons surrounded and captured Dawson's and Barrett's trains.

48 *Ibid.*, p. 16. Colonel E. B. Alexander to Colonel Cooper, Oct. 9, 1857.
49 Brigham Young, "Proclamation," Sept. 5, 1857.

After allowing the bullwhackers to save their outfits, they set fire to the wagons. They also destroyed Simpson's train. The Mormons rounded up the cattle from the three trains. Not long afterward a herd of seven hundred was driven into Salt Lake City. Dawson's and Barrett's bullwhackers walked the twenty miles to Camp Winfield where they reported to James Rupe. The Mormons had burned 300,000 pounds of provisions, which included 2,270 pounds of hams, 93,700 pounds of bacon, 1,400 pounds of sugar, 13,333 pounds of soap and 167,900 pounds of flour, enough to last the entire Army of Utah three months.[50]

General Harney, being familiar with the country west of the Missouri River, was opposed to marching for Utah two months past the usual time for starting. He felt the journey should not be made until early in 1858. An over-eager administration in Washington ruled otherwise, however. This threw the Army of Utah and Majors & Russell's trains so far behind the usual season for travel that by the time South Pass was crossed winter was setting in.

At Camp Winfield, Colonel Alexander ordered an advance toward Salt Lake City along a route recommended by James Bridger, who was acting as guide. This was by way of Soda Springs, on Bear River, and into Salt Lake Valley from the north. Although the route was about a hundred miles longer, it was thought that the Mormons had not burned the grass upon it.[51]

On October 12 they began the march with Majors & Russell Trains 1, 2, 3, 4, 6, and 7 sandwiched into the nine-mile-long column for protection. This arrangement was fatal to the contractors' oxen because they could not find sufficient grass to sustain them. After marching sixty miles the officers freely discussed loading sixty days' rations upon the backs of pack animals, burning the wagon train, and marching into Salt Lake Valley. While still undecided what to do, Colonel Alexander received an order from Colonel A. S. Johnston, who had succeeded General Harney, directing him to turn back to Fontenelle Creek, where grazing was thought to be good. Instead of doing this, Colonel Alexander remained where he was. On October 26 he was ordered to march to a point three miles below the junction of Ham's Fork and Black's Fork.

[50] Herbert Howe Bancroft, *History of Utah*, pp. 513, 515. *A Brief Statement*, p. 15. General A. S. Johnston to Major Irwin McDowell, Oct. 13, 1857. Captain H. F. Clark to Johnston, Nov. 4, 1857. Captain Jesse A. Gove, *The Utah Expedition*, p. 73.

[51] Gove, *The Utah Expedition*, p. 69.

MRS. WILLIAM H. RUSSELL MRS. WILLIAM B. WADDELL

CATHERINE STALCUP MAJORS
First wife of Alexander Majors
(Courtesy of Dr. Ergo Majors)

MRS. ALEXANDER MAJORS
Second wife of Alexander Majors

When the column arrived the oxen in Majors & Russell's trains were completely broken down. On the way they learned that disaster had again struck the unfortunate contractors. Ten miles from Camp Winfield, Stephen Rannchbarger and nine men were herding some nine hundred oxen and a few mules. Porter Rockwell and seventy-five Mormons had swooped out of the mountains and driven the animals off.[52]

On November 3, Colonel Johnston arrived with the rear of the army and a column of Majors & Russell's trains. Three days later he broke camp and marched for Fort Bridger to go into winter quarters. When stretched out along the road the column was eighteen to twenty miles long. Again the trains were sandwiched in among the troops for fear of the Mormons. About noon a snowstorm so heavy the bullwhackers could scarcely see their lead teams swept down upon them. The oxen were turned loose to graze, but they could find nothing to eat. What little grass the Mormons had not burned was buried under seven inches of snow. That night, raiding Saints drove off five hundred more oxen, three hundred and fifty of which belonged to Majors & Russell.[53]

On the morning of November 8 the thermometer stood at 3° below zero. The night before more than half of Majors & Russell's remaining oxen and some of the army's mules had died. Teams were sent back to bring in trains stalled for lack of animals to move them, but many oxen were so weak from starvation they could scarcely walk. The wagons all got in but many of the oxen died under the yoke.

Conditions of the march on the 9th were worse than those of the day before. Again Majors & Russell's oxen died on the road. The Army of Utah was now battling a foe far more dangerous and implacable than Brigham Young's Mormons. The long, frigid Rocky Mountain winter had set in, animals were dying by the hundreds, the soldiers were exposed in the open to subzero weather, and the danger of losing all of the supplies was acute.[54]

The troops remained in camp on November 10 and 11 while Majors & Russell's trains were being moved forward. Nobody thought of advancing upon Salt Lake City now. Fort Bridger, only a few miles away, was their sole hope of refuge. If those great wagons could be gotten there

[52] *A Brief Statement*, pp. 15, 16, 24. Gove, *op. cit.*, p. 69. Bancroft, p. 518. Morehead, "Personal Recollections," in Connelley, *Doniphan's Expedition*, p. 610.

[53] Gove, *op. cit.*, pp. 89, 90. *A Brief Statement*, pp. 16, 17, 19. Morehead, p. 610.

[54] Gove, pp. 92-93.

and their loads stored within its walls, they could make out until spring. They moved only a few miles every other day and devoted the one between to bringing up those precious vehicles. On November 13 they reached the junction of Smith's and Black's Forks. Now only three hundred of Majors & Russell's oxen remained, enough to move one train at a time, but they had to rest every other day.

On the 16th or 17th, the advance reached Fort Bridger, having consumed ten days covering thirty-five miles. For days afterward the remainder of the troops and Majors & Russell's wagons straggled in. Fortunately for the Army of Utah, the Mormons, after seizing the place the preceding May, had erected a stone wall fifteen feet high around the original structure. Attached to this was an enclosure one hundred and eighty feet square with a wall seven and one-half feet high. All buildings constructed of wood had been burned when the Mormons evacuated the place some time before. With about 275 Majors & Russell wagons, besides those belonging to the army, an abundance of good lumber and stout canvas sheets was available. As the trains arrived the supplies were unloaded, stacked against the stone walls and a roof of wood and canvas built over them. Camp was set up around the Fort and the place called Camp Scott.[55]

As the trains were unloaded, James Rupe and Charles R. Morehead Jr., assisted by a force of clerks, checked the contents against the bills of lading. When the checking was finished they were given receipts in full for the eleven trains which had arrived at Fort Bridger. Immediately afterward Rupe and Morehead set out for Fort Leavenworth with two riding and two pack mules. After sundry adventures they arrived at their destination January 26, 1858, having been on the road thirty days and traveling twelve hundred miles. They turned their bills of lading in at the office where a bill against the United States for losses was made out. Summarized, and as later presented to Congress, it read:

Wagons destroyed enroute and left at Camp Scott for want of
    oxen to draw them . . . . $ 48,260.00
1,906 oxen 84,245.50
Outfits for eleven trains 25,696.00
Additional cost for agents, wagon masters, teamsters, etc., during
    winter of 1857-58 . . . . 35,167.15

[55] Gove, *op. cit.*, pp. 92-93, 97. Morehead, *op. cit.*, p. 610.

Three burned trains . . . . $ 72,000.00
Difference between 1857 contract price and cost of transportation
    of 2,264,013 lbs. of supplies to Utah 174,741.80
The same to Fort Laramie 49,679.95
The same to Fort Kearny 3,762.61

                                                     ———————
                                                 $493,553.01 [56]

When Russell, who was in Washington, heard Rupe and Morehead were back at Leavenworth, he telegraphed them to come to that city. Their report must have dismayed him. Now he would see whether Captain Brent's assurance that the government would not allow his firm to suffer loss was worth anything.

Reports coming to Washington by military and other channels convinced the administration that the job in Utah was of far greater magnitude than had been at first supposed. There was the already acute problem of supplying the troops at Fort Bridger. In addition there was the question of reinforcements. On January 11, 1858, it was announced that 3,018 men would be assembled at Fort Leavenworth and sent to Utah.[57]

On January 16, 1858, the partners signed a two-year contract for the transportation of military supplies west of the Missouri River. Again they held a monopoly. This year the name of the firm was changed to Russell, Majors & Waddell. The schedule of rates per one hundred pounds per one hundred miles was as follows:

To Fort Union and intermediate points $3.50 to $4.50; from Fort Union to all other points in New Mexico or any place covered by the agreement $1.50 to $2.20.

To Fort Kearny and intermediate points $1.35 to $4.50; to Salt Lake City or any point in Utah and beyond Fort Laramie $1.80 to $4.50.

These were the basic rates for the first ten million pounds. Those for an additional five million pounds were 25% higher. For all over fifteen million pounds they were 35% higher. The maximum amount for which the firm could be held liable was thirty million pounds.[58]

56 Morehead, *op. cit.,* pp. 611-22. John Bartleson, "Diary," Dec. 1-20, 1867. Charles Byers to Waddell. Jan. 6, 1858.

57 H. R., 35th Cong., 2d sess., Ex. Doc. 2, p. 30. Bancroft, *History of Utah,* p. 521. Russell to Waddell, April 13, 16, 1858.

58 Contract between Russell, Majors & Waddell and Gen. Thomas S. Jesup, Jan. 16, 1858.

When Russell presented the bills of lading that Rupe and Morehead had risked their lives to carry across the snowy, windswept plains in the dead of winter, he was told the War Department had no money with which to pay him. It had already greatly overdrawn its appropriation. When the appropriation was made, no such expense as that involved in the Utah expedition was anticipated. What Russell had feared in the beginning was now a cold, bleak reality. Russell, Majors & Waddell was confronted with the threat of total ruin. Its credit was already impaired, it had suffered losses in wagons, oxen, and equipment amounting to $319,020.81, and the War Department owed it $323,201.64 for transporting supplies under the contract.[59] To further complicate the situation, the business for 1858 required about three times the equipment employed the year before.

Some time in February or March Russell laid the bald, disagreeable truth before Secretary of War John B. Floyd. Since neither the War Department nor the firm had the necessary funds, Russell suggested that he be allowed to draw drafts or acceptances upon the Secretary in anticipation of the firm's earnings for 1858. These were to be used as security with banks or individuals from whom loans would be secured. They were to be regarded as obligations of Russell, Majors & Waddell and none were to be allowed to get back to the War Department. Apparently nobody objected to this plan except Quartermaster General Jesup. He was overruled.[60]

Secretary Floyd also lent his aid in raising money on the acceptances. On March 4, 1858, he wrote letters to George Newbold, President of the Bank of America, in New York, and to August Belmont, frankly confessing the inability of the War Department to pay the contractors for their work in 1857, and asking each of them to honor $200,000 worth of acceptances. Most of these were dated March 25 and were due on the first days of July, August, and September, 1858. The Bank of America declined to take any of them. August Belmont compromised by honoring $100,000 worth. The Bank of the Republic, New York City, took $100,000, and the remainder went to Riggs & Company and Kilgore, Wilson & Company, both of Washington, and to a man by the name of Peckingill. Russell secured more money in Philadelphia, and a Deficiency

[59] H. R., 36th Cong., 2d sess., Report 78, p. 302.
[60] *Ibid.*, pp. 78-80, 82-83.

Bill to relieve the embarrassment of the War Department was introduced in Congress.[61]

While Majors was getting the trains onto the roads in the summer of 1857, Russell formed another of his numerous partnerships. This one, composed of himself, A. B. Miller of Leavenworth, Kansas, and William B. Waddell, was called Miller, Russell & Company. They loaded a train with sutler's goods and sent it across the plains with the Army of Utah, in charge of Miller. Although this firm had no technical relationship to Russell, Major & Waddell, it nevertheless proved to be a heavy liability. Miller opened a store at Camp Scott and moved into Salt Lake Valley when the army entered it in the spring of 1858. He secured a warehouse 100 by 44 feet and rented two store buildings to house his goods. In addition he opened stores at Millersville and Camp Floyd. One was also probably kept at Camp Scott to supply emigrants. By the fall of 1858, the concern owed Russell, Majors & Waddell $200,000.[62]

When the contract for 1858 and 1859 was written, a clause provided that an additional starting point on the Missouri River north of Fort Leavenworth should be chosen. The honor fell to Nebraska City, a scrawny little river town one hundred and fifty miles upstream.

Majors, his first wife having died January 14, 1856, had married Susan Wetzel of Jackson County, Missouri, March 23, 1857.[63] He now moved his family and retinue of slaves from his home south of Westport to the new location. Russell closed his house in Lexington, moved to Leavenworth, and built a larger one.

While Majors was transforming sleepy little Nebraska City into a hustling river port of importance, Russell and his friends in Washington were heroically working against time to jam the Deficiency Bill through Congress. Both houses passed resolutions calling upon Secretary Floyd to produce all contracts relative to the Utah expedition. During the debates the whole Mormon difficulty was thoroughly aired, the Administration was savagely attacked for having sent soldiers to Utah at all, and Russell, Majors & Waddell were held up to public view as chiseling contractors. When the bill passed in May the firm had been thoroughly

---

61 *Ibid.*, pp. 30, 302-304.

62 *Record Book* J, No. 1, Lafayette County, Mo., p. 383. *Leavenworth Journal*, Feb. 19, 1864. Charles Byers to Waddell, Jan. 6, 1858.

63 Contract between Russell, Majors & Waddell and Jesup. *Marriage Record* 4, Jackson County, Mo., p. 7.

discredited, but funds to pay what the War Department owed it for work in 1857 were available.

Majors was in Washington to assist Russell early in 1858. On his way home in March, he stopped at Westport to subcontract twenty-five trainloads of military supplies to eighteen private freighters. The army rented a warehouse on the river front at Westport Landing and made that place a starting point also. It is probable that other contracts were also let, for the day after the first ones were signed Robert B. Bradford wrote Waddell that Majors had let contracts for twelve hundred loads, enough to make up forty-eight trains. If Bradford was correct, this strategy relieved the partners of an investment of about half a million dollars. If not, they saved about half that amount on those he did let. Russell, Majors & Waddell agreed to furnish wagons, chains, ox yokes, wagon covers, and other equipment at customary prices, and to pay $19.60 per one hundred pounds per one hundred miles to Salt Lake City and $18.00 to Fort Bridger. The contractors furnished their own oxen, bullwhackers, and whatever else was required, and took their pay from the first money due the firm on the loads they carried. The remuneration was about equal to what the War Department paid on the first ten million pounds. Apparently the object was to arrange it so that these cargoes would come under the 25% and 35% increases. This would insure a handsome profit without any risk whatever.[64]

[64] Contract between Russell, Majors & Waddell and sub-contractors, March 30, 1858. Robert B. Bradford to Waddell, March 31, 1858. Russell to Waddell & Russell, March 31, April 13, 1858. John W. Waddell to William B. Waddell, March 27, April 13, 1858.

IV

HOW THEY DID IT

I N MAY both the town of Leavenworth and the nearby Fort were scenes of glorious activity. White-topped wagons, greased and carrying extra timbers lashed in place beneath the boxes, stood in long rows between the town and the Fort. Out upon the prairie, oxen quietly fed under the watchful eyes of mounted stock tenders. Every one of the oxen wore the Russell, Majors & Waddell brand, the ox yoke. Most of them were broken to work, but some were not. Over by the corrals sweating bullwhackers were busy making up their teams, yoking them together, and allowing them to become accustomed to each other. If a young one was to be broken and trained he was yoked with an old one, and, their tails tied together, they were turned loose so that the youngster might learn how to conduct himself in that situation. When he had learned to walk quietly beside his companion, they were hitched to a wagon and driven about for a while.

Up at the Fort soldiers on fatigue duty unloaded supplies from steamboats or took them out of warehouses and placed them in wagons under the watchful eye of the wagon master. This was highly important work and had to be done just right. A mistake in loading might cause the cargo to shift going up or down hill and delay an entire train for hours while it was being reloaded. At the rear end of the wagon, where the goods were lifted in, stood a clerk from the quartermaster's department writing down upon a bill of lading the contents and weight of each item. When the loading was finished a copy was given to the wagon master and another sent to Russell, Majors & Waddell's office.

Upon leaving the starting point the wagon master was given a copy of the bills of lading and a "train book." This little volume, solidly bound in leather, served much the same purpose as a ship's log at sea. The names of the bullwhackers, stock tenders, or any other persons accompanying the train were written down in it. It also served as a ledger for keeping accounts with the employees. Since the bullwhackers carried very little with them on the road, they bought such things as tobacco,

27

boots, handkerchiefs, clothing, or whatever else they might need. These purchases were charged against them in the train book and whatever they owed the firm was deducted at the end of the journey. When the train returned to Leavenworth the book was handed in at the office and the accounts quickly balanced. It also served as a kind of diary of the trip, for the wagon master was required to record anything of more than ordinary importance in it.

By 1858, freight wagons for the Plains had become more or less standardized. Moreover, experience had taught the manufacturers how to build them in order to obtain the best possible service upon the road. To begin with, all of the wood which went into them was thoroughly seasoned. This meant that it was kept lying in sheds for at least two years after it was sawed. Special attention was given the wood which went into the wheels. The hubs, spokes, and felloes were generally made of white oak but Osage orange (plain hedge) wood was also used. Extreme care was exercised in the manufacture of the wheels, for a wagon upon the road was no better than its wheels. Before starting on a trip each one of them was carefully inspected. If the iron tire seemed a bit loose it was taken off, heated, and reset. On long journeys this was sometimes done on the road. The axles were made of strong white oak. Some made of iron were tried out in the late 1840's but were quickly abandoned because if one was broken or bent on the road it was impossible to repair it.

The bodies, capable of holding as much as five thousand pounds, were of light but strong construction. Their bottoms were slightly curved to prevent loads from shifting in going up or down hill. The front extended forward like the prow of a ship, but the rear was square with an end-gate which was hinged at the bottom and opened outward. Sockets along the side accommodated hickory bows, over which was stretched a white Osnaburg cover or sheet. When properly adjusted, stretched tight, and tied down, it formed a perfectly weatherproof covering for the goods it carried. In contrast to the emigrant wagon, the freight wagon carried no one. The bullwhacker walked, on the left hand side as a rule, but occasionally he sat or stood upon the rear end of the tongue where it joined the front hounds.

A box on the side contained a few tools and underneath the body a number of pieces of hardwood were slung for repairs upon the road.

In all the history of transportation no vehicle was ever better adapted to the use for which it was intended. They were comparatively light for their bulk, amazingly sturdy, and capable of standing up under severe punishment. With reasonable care, they easily withstood several round trips to Santa Fe or Salt Lake City before being retired to a farm somewhere, there to render further service indefinitely.

With Russell, Majors & Waddell the movement and management of trains upon the road was reduced to a system expressed in "Rules and Regulations." [65] These were printed in the form of leaflets and pamphlets and distributed among the men. They were also included in the train books. The first rule bluntly stated that "Swearing, gambling, and intemperance will not be allowed, either in camp or on the plains." As before remarked, this rule meant exactly what it said. Old bullwhackers who had become the victims of bad habits were expected to abandon them and new men not to form them.

Some of the rules were explicit, especially those relating to the handling of the oxen.

When about corraling, caution your men against exciting the cattle, by hallooing and cracking whips at them. They should be so careful that a long, deep-toned "whoa" would stop their teams in the exact spot required. . . . .

If water be near the camp, let the cattle feed to it instead of being driven there. But if necessary to drive them, let them linger some time about the water, so that they all may become cool and have a chance to satisfy their thirst. . . . .

In driving cattle to the corral, men enough must be employed to encircle them and drive them directly in, and when at a distance from the camp, drive them very slowly, as fast driving injures them greatly.

No man should begin yoking before the cattle have had two or three minutes to become quieted in, then all should enter and yoke in a quiet gentle manner. First yoke the wheelers and chain them to the front wheel outside the corral, or hitch them to the tongue; secondly yoke the leaders and fasten them to the wagon, on the inside, and so on until the whole team is yoked, and hitched up, when they will be taken out of the corral and hitched to the wagon. . . . .

After leaving the corral, do not travel more than ½ to 1 mile before stopping 8 or 10 minutes for the cattle to breathe and urinate, particularly if the weather is warm and cattle full. . . . .

[65] Russell, Majors & Waddell, *Rules and Regulations for the Government of Outfits; Train Book;* "Instructions to Wagon-masters."

Drive the oxen into the corral in the morning as soon as the teamsters can see to yoke, and travel until 10 A.M., varying an hour more or less, according to camping ground. Remain in camp 2 or 3 hours, and then make the evening drive. These rules are conducting a loaded train.

The same rules may be observed in an empty train, in regard to hitching up as early as you can see, but in this case travel until 7 or 9 o'clock A.M., according [to] the time of getting off. As a general thing, an empty train should not travel more than from 6 to 8 miles; and a loaded train from seven to ten, according to camping ground. The hands should cook and eat in such time as to enable the train to hitch up again in an hour and a half to two hours, when you will make another drive of from 6 to 8 miles, and then remain in camp 3 to 4 hours, as this is the warm part of the day, and this will give animals and men a chance to rest; then hitch up, always taking your stoutest cattle for the teams, and make an evening drive, which will sometimes throw you a little after dark in coming to camp. When arrived turn out your cattle, put out your guard, and let the rest of the hands go to bed. This will give hands two meals a day, which is sufficient for men on the plains, as they eat hearty and have strong diet. . . . .

Do not allow the men to whip their teams at all. The use of profane language is strictly forbidden. We expect our trains to observe the Sabbath, and whenever an opportunity occurs to hear preaching, embrace it. We want our men to pay due respect to all persons they meet on the road, whether Indians or whites, as many difficulties often occur from abuse and insult offered to inoffensive people.

Wagon wheels were kept greased at all times, lock chains, used to stop the wheels from rolling while going downhill, were to be well wrapped with gunny sacks before putting on, to prevent injury to the spokes and felloes; and a little grease was put on the gooseneck of each ox chain and yoke staple at least once a week. In corralling the train the lead wagon and half the others were stopped on the right-hand side of the camp site in the form of a half circle. The middle wagon swung to the left, and with the remainder behind it formed the other half. In a few minutes the corral was formed with the teams on the inside. By this simple device the train was converted into an enclosure into which the oxen could be driven when the time came to start again. Every time it was stopped long enough to unhitch the animals and turn them loose the corral was formed, no matter where it might be. When far out upon the plains the corral also served as an excellent means of defense against possible Indian attacks. If necessary the oxen could be driven inside and the opening at each end closed. Under this arrangement a train could withstand a long siege against vastly superior forces.

One wagon in the train was known as the "kitchen wagon." It was loaded with food supplies and camp equipment for the men. Unless the trip was too long, this wagon carried sufficient provisions to last them for a round trip. Their diet was indeed "strong." It consisted of flour, corn meal, bacon, pickled pork, dried fruits and vegetables, beans, dried corn, coffee, etc. Sometimes they got fresh meat by killing a buffalo or other game, but since Russell, Majors & Waddell's trains moved according to a rigid schedule hunting was not encouraged.

Before starting, the bullwhackers were divided into messes of five or six men each, one of whom served as cook. The others took care of his oxen for him. Each was expected to have a "chip sack" attached to the side of his wagon into which he tossed buffalo chips or other fuel which came his way during the day. Equipment for cooking was simple and limited to a pot or two, a skillet, a coffeepot, and a Dutch oven for baking bread. Each man had an iron knife, spoon, fork, tin cup, and a plate which he washed and scrubbed with sand after each meal.

When starting, each man was issued a Colt's six-shooter, a rifle, and ammunition. They were required to keep them clean, in working order, and handy, although no attack by Indians upon a Russell, Majors & Waddell train is recorded. Perhaps the red lords of the mountains and plains had a healthy respect for the hard-bitten men, who were expert with both firearms and bull-whip.

Alexander Majors could not be kept at home when the time for starting the trains came. His habit was to ride back and forth along the road, visiting each in turn, and keeping an eye upon things. The wagon masters and bullwhackers liked this, for they knew he spoke their language and understood the hardships and conditions under which they worked and lived. He sat down upon the ground beside a pot of savory stew cooked over buffalo chips, filled his own tin plate like everyone else, and scrubbed his utensils. When night came he unstrapped his blankets from his saddle and found his bed upon the ground under a wagon along with the rest of the crew. On Sunday he held a church service, led in the singing of hymns, and preached. None of these discourses have been preserved, but they must have been noteworthy for their simple, unquestioning faith and honest straightforward common sense. He had read his Bible so consistently and pondered its fundamental spiritual and moral principles so thoroughly that he had much to say to these hard working men whose lot he shared. And Alexander Majors could both read and write well. Although not a highly educated man, judged by academic standards, he was nevertheless quite literate. He read a great deal, and his letters, written in a firm, strong hand disclose a considerable degree of ability. The myth that he could neither read nor write is pure fiction and without the slightest foundation in fact. After all, he wrote a book.

V

THE LEAVENWORTH & PIKE'S PEAK
EXPRESS COMPANY

HILE RUSSELL, Majors & Waddell's wagons were churning the dust along the road to Salt Lake City in the summer and fall of 1858, events which were to exert a great influence upon the lives and fortunes of the partners were transpiring far to the southwest along the front range of the Rocky Mountains. The principal event was the discovery of gold in what was then called the "Pike's Peak" region of western Kansas. The news reached Leavenworth when a prospector walked into a bank in August or September with a goose quill full of gold dust which he said he had found on Cherry Creek. That touched off more excitement than the town had known in many a day. As usual, when someone said "Gold!" daring fortune hunters made a frenzied dash toward its alleged place of origin.

At the first mention of the shining metal, Russell, like everyone else, pricked up his ears. He talked with anyone he could find who had been to that region—there were not many—and did a great deal of solid thinking. Not that he was interested in joining the stampede of gold hunters. He loved clean linen, dainty food, and a comfortable bed to sleep in at night too well for that. But other factors in the case, such as transportation, merchandising, and the express business were within his particular field. If the new discovery turned out to be even half as valuable as that in California a decade before, there would be ample opportunity for making money without digging it out of the ground or washing it out of a creek bed.

During the fall of 1858, Russell and Waddell, and possibly Majors, held long conversations concerning the new El Dorado. One Sunday afternoon General William Larimer, resident of Leavenworth, and his son William H. H., members of a party organized for the purpose of prospecting for gold, called upon Russell to seek his advice concerning travel

33

upon the plains. It was also General Larimer's plan to organize a town company when he got there. Since this latter project was very much in Russell's line, that, and the possibility of starting a stage line to "Pike's Peak" was discussed. Before the conversation ended it was understood that Russell should have one share in the town company. Consequently, when it was organized on Cherry Creek on November 22, 1858, as the Denver City Town Company his name was entered as one of the original shareholders.[66] This gave him about thirty acres in the heart of what quickly became the metropolis of the Rocky Mountains and the capital of the state of Colorado.

Back in Leavenworth the three partners discussed the proposition of sending a trainload of goods to the new town and opening a store. Granting that gold was to be found there in paying quantities, the hordes of people who would flock there would be eager customers for anything in the way of provisions, clothing, tools, etc. Before they did anything, however, Russell set out for the East in the latter part of November. Writing from Chicago, where he made a tour of the city and appraised it from the speculator's angle, he said, "Pike's Peak will rage next year and no mistake. We must keep our eyes open and try to make enough out of it to cover our extraordinary losses next season arising from high prices of cattle and wagons. . . . I am for sending a cargo of supplies out there." [67]

The freighting monopoly Russell, Majors & Waddell had enjoyed since 1855 was certain to come under close scrutiny. Jealous rival firms alone would have brought that to pass. The Utah affair, which was never popular with the people, constituted a golden opportunity for anti-Administration fault finders. This bore fruit late in 1858 or early in 1859 in the passage of a resolution in the House of Representatives calling upon Secretary Floyd for a copy of the contract with the firm. The partners, irked by the whole situation and knowing themselves to be sailing dangerous waters, decided to chuck the whole business overboard. In a letter to the Secretary they tendered their resignation as government contractors for the transportation of military supplies to both New Mexico and Utah on the sole condition that the War Department buy their equipment at a price fixed by a board of appraisers. Secretary Floyd re-

[66] Larimer, *Reminiscences*, p. 97.
[67] Russell to Waddell, Nov. 24, 1858.

fused to accept their resignation, which, in the light of later events, was unfortunate for the partners.[68]

1212945

During the winter of 1858-59 John S. Jones went to Washington. At that time he was engaged in the private freighting business and was advertising in the New York newspapers that he would send fifty trains of twenty-five wagons each to "Pike's Peak" from Westport and Atchison, Kansas. While in the capital he met Russell. Naturally they discussed the gold diggings and prospects for business there. They thought about the people flocking across the plains in huge numbers and their imaginations were stirred. Anyone wishing to make the trip had to either provide a wagon and team or attach himself to a party which already had one. This was not always an easy matter, for most of the parties were made up before reaching the Missouri River. Getting back was worse. Most of the eastbound travelers were bankrupt and their outfits quite nondescript.

The distance from the Missouri River to Denver by way of the California Crossing was 635 miles. That was a long way, but to men accustomed to thinking in terms of the miles to Santa Fe and Salt Lake City it was not so far after all. By plodding ox train it was a matter of only thirty-five to forty days at the most. Since the miles were not too many and the number of people who wanted to go would probably be large, a stage line was desirable.

Early in February 1859, a company called "The Leavenworth & Pike's Peak Express Company" was organized. Russell was president and Jones general manager. Other members and stockholders were the president's eldest son, John W., who was made secretary, Luther R. Smoot, and Benjamin F. Ficklin, who probably acted as route agent. Forty shares at $5,000 each were issued. Russell contributed $20,000 in cash.[69] Jones probably invested a like amount.

Ficklin had gone west with the United States Wagon Road surveying party of one hundred men, under William F. McGraw, to lay out a road from South Pass to Salt Lake City. When the work was stopped by the Mormon difficulty, McGraw placed his equipment at the disposal of Colonel Johnston and released his men. Some fifty or sixty

[68] Russell, Majors & Waddell to John B. Floyd, Jan. 8, 1859.

[69]. Byers to Waddell, Feb. 4, 1859. Contract between Russell, Majors & Waddell and John S. Jones, et al., Oct. 29, 1859. *Kansas Historical Quarterly*, XIII, 168. Russell to Waddell, April 12, 1859. Jones, Russell & Company, Balance Sheet, Nov. 1859.

enlisted as soldiers, but most of the others made their way back home. Ficklin served as Deputy United States Marshal for a brief period, then entered the service of Colonel Johnston. He made a trip into the Flat-head Indian country in the middle of the winter of 1857-58 to buy beef cattle and mules. Upon returning, about the middle of April 1858, he set out for the East with dispatches.[70]

Russell expected Waddell, and possibly Majors, to join him in his stagecoach adventure although he had not consulted them. When Wad-dell heard about it he wrote Russell a series of blistering letters. He railed against his partner for involving his associates in the scheme, flatly refused to have anything to do with it, criticized contracts made in Wash-ington, and complained against Russell's long absences from home. These letters threw Russell upon the defensive and compelled him to take time out for long, meticulous explanations which only served to further in-furiate Waddell. Most of these fiery complaints were addressed to St. Louis and forwarded to Washington where Russell received five of them on April 12, 1858. This was too much. Seizing his pen he spoke his mind.

I had hoped that I could have some peace during my irksome sojourn here. . . . I took it for granted that you would join me in the Emigrant line . . . . and also my interest in the Express Company. . . . . This is the last letter answering complaints that I will write. If you have spoken of my *large* (as you call them) adventures in Pike's Peak to outsiders I will thank you to disabuse the public mind. For if I find it so on my return and no correction *I will* most assuredly publish the transaction under my own name and explain the reason which impel[s] me so to do. I am not a reckless gambler and I will not be so posted.

Disquieting and painful though the thought of being "posted" as a "reckless gambler" may have been to Russell, that was what had hap-pened. In both Lexington and Leavenworth it was common talk that he had involved himself and partners in a wild-cat speculative enterprise. Whether the story was set afloat by Waddell, Majors, competitors, credi-tors, friends, or enemies made no difference. That was what was being said. Somebody, of course, told his wife about it and she poured out her indignation in a letter to him. Russell wrote to Waddell on April 17, 1858:

[70] Gove, *The Utah Expedition*, pp. 73, 215, 239, 240. Nebraska Historical Society *Publications*, XX, 321. Albert G. Brown, Warrants for Arrest, Nov. 7, 24, 1857.

Dr. Joseph L. Cartright
(*Courtesy of Mrs. A. N. Adams*)

John S. Jones
(*Courtesy of Mrs. John Wall*)

My poor wife writes me from Lexington that she is in deep distress, that my partners have reported that I was reckless and gone into Pike's Peak to a ruinous extent [and] that my stay in Washington was uncalled for and unnecessary. . . . I care not who started such reports (I trust you or Mr. M[ajors] did not) I pronounce them false calumniators and liars and will on my return hold any man accountable who has falsely slandered me.[71]

The matter seems to have been dropped here by all parties concerned, but the attitude of criticism and complaint against Russell and his methods in Waddell's mind never abated. Always it lurked beneath the surface, ready to break forth in recriminations as opportunity afforded. If Waddell's refusal to have anything to do with the Leavenworth & Pike's Peak Express Company discouraged Russell in the slightest degree there is no evidence of it. Although there was no connection between the new concern and Russell, Majors & Waddell, he knew that whatever prestige the freighting company enjoyed would constitute one of his most reliable assets.

The launching of this express company was the second disastrous mistake Russell made. Had he resisted the temptation to join Jones in it and worked solely to repair Russell, Majors & Waddell's damaged credit the firm might have succeeded. His action further undermined its financial standing, earned for himself the reputation of being a reckless gambler and involved him and his partners in a series of catastrophic events which in the end brought total ruin.

Work toward putting the line into operation began immediately. Knowing that competition would quickly appear, especially if the venture were a success, Russell and Jones determined to lay out a new road to the Rocky Mountains along the shortest possible route. The task of finding it, marking it, and building stations along the way was committed to Colonel William J. Preston of Leavenworth. His party set out March 15, 1859, along the military road to Fort Riley. Passing through Easton, Ozawkie, and Indianola, they struck the Kaw River at Silver Lake. From here they followed that stream through St. Marys, Louisville, and Manhattan to Junction City. On the way they located seven stations.[72]

Leaving Junction City, still following the Kaw River, they crossed Chapman Creek, then turned northwest up its right bank, crossed the

71 Russell to Waddell, April 17, 1859.
72 *Kansas Historical Quarterly,* XIII, 165.

headwaters of Pipe Creek, struck the Solomon River and followed it to the head of Limestone Creek. Here the route was later joined by the trail from Atchison. From this point they traveled slightly northwest to the Republican River, locating seven more stations on the road. Here they swung to the southwest along the right bank of the South Fork of the Republican, later crossing to the other side, and arrived at Big Sandy Creek, a tributary of the Arkansas River, having marked the sites for seven additional stations. Following along the north bank of Big Sandy, they traveled northwest until they reached Bijou Creek and thence along its east bank to Denver. By prearrangement, no doubt, they stopped at the cabin occupied by General Larimer and his son. Two more stations were located along this section of the road, making a total of twenty-seven, including those at Leavenworth and Denver. The party made the outbound trip in twenty-three days, spent three in the lusty young town, and set out on their return to Leavenworth on April 9. They arrived home on the 25th.[73]

On March 28 a train of twenty wagons set out from Leavenworth to build and equip the stations. Another, with the same number of wagons and carrying one hundred persons, including the families of station keepers, left on April 1. It was intended that tents should be used at the stations until permanent houses of logs, sod, or adobe could be constructed. The stations were about twenty-five miles apart, and it was planned that six men should be on duty at each, four drivers and two stock tenders. The drivers contracted to work twelve months. Half their wages were to be held back each payday, and the money would be forfeited if a man broke his contract. It was estimated that twenty-five wagons would be required in service the year round to supply the stations with forage and provisions.[74]

While Colonel Preston was laying out the road and locating stations, John S. Jones was busy at his office in the Planter's Hotel getting wagons, bullwhackers, and drivers for the stages ready. In addition to the men needed for wagons being loaded with supplies for the stations, others were required for the freight line Jones had announced in the New York newspapers. This company had no connection with the stage line except as an associate institution for carrying freight.

[73] *Kansas Historical Quarterly*, XIII, 173-177.
[74] *Ibid.*, pp. 171-174.

When Russell laid the proposition of starting the stage line before Alexander Majors, the latter promptly vetoed it. "I told them," Majors said, "that I could not consent to do so, for it would be impossible to make such a venture, at such an early period of the development of the country, a paying proposition, and urgently advised them to let the enterprise alone." [75] When all the factors involved in the situation, in relation to the gold discoveries and the affairs of Russell, Majors & Waddell, are analyzed and weighed, the only possible verdict is that Majors and Waddell were right.

In setting up and financing the express company, Russell followed his usual custom of relying principally upon credit. One thousand Kentucky mules, about fifty new Concord coaches, and other equipment were bought with notes payable in ninety days. It is likely that Jones also contributed $20,000 to the concern, for when Russell, Majors & Waddell took the company over its balance sheet showed an item of $23,000 due him. If Smoot, Ficklin, and John W. Russell invested anything, no record remains of it.

[75] Majors, *Seventy Years on the Frontier*, p. 164.

VI

ALL ABOARD FOR PIKE'S PEAK!

N MONDAY MORNING, April 18, 1859, two of the Concord coaches, each drawn by four of the best mules the Company owned, stood before the door of the office in Planter's Hotel in Leavenworth.[76] A crowd of curious, excited people filled the street and overflowed down the steep hillside toward the levee. John S. Jones moved among them with an air of happy proprietorship, receiving congratulations, looking the equipages over with an experienced eye, and giving last minute instructions. William H. Russell was not there. Instead he was in New York, pouting because of Waddell's stern, acrid remonstrances and the accusation of being a "reckless gambler." Without a doubt, many people in the crowd that morning shared those sentiments.

At least ten persons, nine of whom were through-passengers from Leavenworth to Denver, immortalized themselves by making the first trip. Among them were Beverly D. Williams, Dr. John M. Fox, general agent for the company in Denver, Colonel Preston, and another member of the surveying party. The trip was to be made partly in the daytime and partly at night, with stops at the stations for changes of mules, drivers, and for meals. When they traveled at night the passengers slept in the coaches, if they could. At first they became weary, then cramped, and at last numb, if they were lucky.

The two trail-blazing coaches rolled along toward the sunset, passing station after station without accident or incident worthy of more than casual mention. Several bands of Indians, who had heard the news concerning Russell's "painted wagons" greeted the travelers with friendly sentiments as they rocked along. On Saturday, May 7, they completed their journey and halted in the town of Denver. The trip had consumed twenty days. A large crowd surged around the coaches with wild demonstrations of joy. Everybody had been depressed, public auctions of the effects of discouraged miners were frequent and many were taking the

[76] *Kansas Historical Quarterly*, XIII, 188, 190.

road back home. They all declared that Russell was a public benefactor and Leavenworth the "greatest city in the East." The young *Rocky Mountain News* issued an extra from its office in the middle of Cherry Creek in honor of the memorable event.[77]

A log cabin without windows, on the corner of Blake and F Street, was secured and was occupied as an office for about two weeks. Here Dr. Fox and Martin Fields, postmaster, and young William H. H. Larimer, assistant, set up business. Nelson Sargent was route agent for the Western Division, of one hundred and fifty miles. Within a day or two the Denver City Town Company donated nine original shares to the Leavenworth & Pike's Peak Express Company and one each to Russell and Beverly D. Williams. The establishment of the express company in Denver assured that town's pre-eminence over its rival, Auraria, on the opposite bank of Cherry Creek. Williams looked the infant city over and made the choices of lots for himself, the company, and possibly Russell.[78]

While the first two coaches were backtracking toward the Missouri River, the people of Leavenworth were busy planning a mammoth celebration. As they approached the town on May 20, a reception committee composed of men and women drove out along the trail to meet them. Bouquets of roses were presented to the surprised drivers and passengers. Next day a long parade, made up of two brass bands, three fire companies, and people on foot, on horse back, in wagons, buggies, and carriages wound through the streets. That night a great dinner and ball was given at the Planter's Hotel.[79]

The work of supplying the stations was one of considerable proportions. Grain and hay for the mules and provisions for employees and travelers had to be transported in wagons. The company seems to have had three trains of these in service. At first, and until the coaches began running singly, each station had to provide corrals for at least twelve mules besides a number of horses. The latter, unless they were in constant use, could be grazed but the former had to have corn and hay in unstinted quantities. The number of persons at stations varied from four

---

[77] *Ibid.*, p. 395. In order to preserve neutrality between the contending villages of Auraria and Denver, the office was built on posts set in the creek bed.

[78] Larimer, *Reminiscences*, pp. 173-177. *Kansas Historical Quarterly.* XIII, 188, 214. Robert B. Bradford to Waddell, Oct. 19, 1859.

[79] *Kansas Historical Quarterly,* XIII, 192, 193-194.

drivers and a stock tender at a "swing station" to whole families at "home stations."

Data upon which to base an estimate of the cost of operating the line is both slender and fragmentary. Enough exists, however, to serve as an index to the task of financing that Russell had undertaken. Drivers were paid $40 to $75 per month and board, stock tenders $40 to $50, carpenters $75, harness makers and blacksmiths $100 to $125, division agents $100 to $125 and messengers $62.50. When the company had been in operation forty-three days, John S. Jones had an estimate made up of wages due employees for the next two and a half months. It listed 175 men, whose pay varied from $25 to $125 per month. The total was $14,437. When the wages of officers, clerks, bullwhackers, and wagon masters, the forage and provisions for the stations, and the other numberless items of expense were added, the total was about $1,000 per day. No wonder Majors and Waddell emphatically turned thumbs down upon the proposition.[80]

The departure of the coaches from Leavenworth on May 25 proved to be considerably more of a historical event than anyone expected. Albert D. Richardson, correspondent for the *Boston Journal,* was one of the passengers. The company was delighted to "dead-head" him through to Denver and receive its payment in the articles he planned to write about the trip. At Junction City, Horace Greeley, famed tow-headed editor of the *New York Tribune,* joined him for the remainder of the way. This was the first trip upon the Great Plains for both and nothing they saw, heard, or experienced was commonplace or uninteresting. Both amply repaid their hosts by writing reams of fascinating descriptions of the route, life in a stagecoach, and stories about the "diggings" in the mountains.

The coach bearing them was the last over the new route. They arrived in Denver June 6 and Russell's attempt to pioneer a road from the Missouri River to the Rocky Mountains ended. Today the exact location of the trail across much of central and western Kansas is difficult to find. No permanent stations were built and no latitude and longitude for the stopping places recorded. These things, like many another secret of those romantic days, lie locked forever in the mysterious, brooding silence of the Great Plains.

[80] D. R. Risley, Estimate of Wages, May 30, 1859. Frank A. Root and William E. Connelley, *The Overland Stage to California,* p. 155.

About a week before the first coaches rolled out of Leavenworth for Denver, Russell assumed another heavy liability. On May 11 he bought the contract of J. M. Hockaday & Company to transport United States mail from the Missouri River to Salt Lake City, which was to run until November 30, 1860. The purchase price was $50,000, plus the appraised value of the company's equipment, such as houses, corrals, farming utensils, mules, coaches, wagons, harness, etc. This brought the sale price up to $144,000. Payment was to be made by allowing Hockaday & Company to collect the current quarterly pay from the Post Office Department, $23,750, and Jones' and Russell's acceptances for the remainder. These were dated May 15, 1859, to fall due as follows: $36,250, September 1-10, 1859; and $15,000, September 15, 1859. The balance was to be paid in three equal instalments at four, eight, and twelve months from May 15, 1859. The first was due four months after the appraisal of the property and the other two in eight and twelve months. It was further agreed that the line would run through Atchison, Kansas.[81]

Among other things the Hockaday & Company contract provided that the mail should be carried once a week from St. Joseph, Missouri, via Forts Kearny and Laramie, to Salt Lake City and back, in twenty-one days, in carriages or covered wagons drawn by four mules or horses. The original contract called for pay of $190,000 per year, but the Postmaster General had reduced it to $130,000, effective July 1, 1859. For some reason this transaction was kept secret for a time. Therefore, it was negotiated by Luther R. Smoot and Hockaday himself. Smoot and Hockaday were made assignees for Hockaday & Company and Jones and Russell the beneficiaries.[82]

Since the Hockaday & Company contract called for a line from St. Joseph to Salt Lake City along a portion of the Oregon Trail, Russell and Jones decided to abandon the new stage route just opened and send the coaches to Denver by way of Fort Kearny and the Upper California Crossing of the Platte River. Late in June the original route was abandoned and service temporarily interrupted while the change was made under the direction of Beverly D. Williams. The new road ran from Leavenworth northwest to Kennekuk, where it joined the trail from Atchison and St. Joseph. From here it followed the old military road to

81 *Kansas Historical Quarterly*, XIII, 486, 487 n.
82 *Ibid.*, p. 488.

Fort Kearny. Thence it ran along the south bank of the Platte to its forks, then up the South Fork to the Upper California Crossing where Julesburg was founded. There the coaches for Salt Lake City crossed the stream and ascended Lodge Pole Creek. The road to Denver continued up the South Fork to St. Vrain's Fort and from that place south to its destination.

The stations, varying from sixteen to forty-three miles apart, were set up as permanent locations, some of them at or near ranches or trading posts already in operation. Everything possible was done to insure the comfort and convenience of the wayfarers. The first coach over the new route, with at least six passengers aboard, left Leavenworth on July 2 and arrived at Denver on the morning of July 9. The trip required seven days and everyone was delighted with the service. They found good eating houses at the stations, some of which served such splendid meals as to throw "many an Eastern brag house in the shade."

Alexander Majors said that Hockaday & Company had only a few light, cheap stages, a few mules, no stations along the route to Salt Lake City, and traveled the same team hundreds of miles, stopping every few hours to let the animals graze. Jones and Russell changed all that by putting on better equipment and building stations along the roads to both Salt Lake City and Denver. Under the management of Hockaday & Company the line was divided into three Divisions—St. Joseph to Julesburg, under Charles W. Wiley; Julesburg to South Pass, under Joseph A. Slade; and South Pass to Salt Lake City, under James E. Bromley. All of these men became employees of the Leavenworth & Pike's Peak Express Company when the transfer was made.[83]

The question of fares over the Leavenworth & Pike's Peak Express Company's line to Denver was a rather difficult one, there being neither precedent nor competition. Other concerns were advertising for passengers to the gold mines, but they were proposing to transport them in slow-moving ox trains. The fare each way was fixed at $125, with meals extra. These latter, which went up in cost and down in quality the farther west one traveled, were not designed to tickle the palate of an epicurean. There were twenty-five eating stations between the Missouri River and Denver. Through eastern Kansas and as far west as Marysville, vegetables in season, eggs, chickens, butter and milk, ham, bacon, prairie

[83] *Kansas Historical Quarterly*, XIII, 498 n.

chickens, and occasionally buffalo meat were served. Beyond Marysville and on the Platte River the fare was more rugged. It still included ham and bacon, but dried fruits and vegetables made their appearance. Along the Little Blue River roasted wild turkey and antelope meat were common. The cost of a meal varied from fifty cents on the eastern end to a dollar and a half on the western.

When the express company began operations it was the object of extravagant praise by the people of the Rocky Mountains. This honeymoon type of attitude was, however, unable to withstand the wear and tear of the weeks which followed. At first the immigrants, who had been influenced by guidebooks printed in Leavenworth and unwise advertising by newspapers of that place, arrived in Denver complaining that they had been deceived as to the route's advantages. Of course they vented their anger upon the express company. After securing the Hockaday & Company mail contract and the transfer of the line to the Platte River route, the *Rocky Mountain News* severely criticized the company for charging twenty-five cents for carrying a letter. These, and probably other matters, so rankled in the public mind that by the latter part of September, 1859, Robert B. Bradford was writing home to Waddell that there was much excitement about it all. Some six weeks later he was of the opinion that the office or its agency in Denver was a curse to any man connected with it.

Not long after taking charge Bradford instituted a system of receiving prepaid orders for small parcels of goods and forwarding them to Leavenworth to be sent out by express. This worked very well until John W. Russell took over the office at that place and began charging an additional five percent commission. This caused Bradford to discontinue the service which, together with an advance of freight rates to seventy-five cents per pound, added to the unpopularity of the company.

When the line to Salt Lake City was first put into operation, John S. Jones acted as route superintendent. This arrangement proving impracticable, Beverly D. Williams was appointed to succeed him. Late in 1859 Benjamin F. Ficklin assumed the duties of the office. By this time the affairs of the company were in a bad way, expenses not being met, stock was regularly disappearing from the stations and a condition bordering upon chaos prevailed. Understanding the source of much of the trouble, Ficklin addressed himself to the rigorous task of house cleaning.

The first item on his agenda was that of driving thieves out of the company and off the line.

One of the new stations established on the Platte River route was at Julesburg. Here Jules Beni, or Reni as it is sometimes spelled, known upon the plains and in the mountains as "Old Jules," had established a trading post. Although employed as agent and station keeper he kept around him a gang of thugs through whom he preyed upon the company. Ficklin's first step toward remedying this situation was to instruct Joseph A. Slade to discharge Old Jules. This so angered the old trader that he waylaid Slade and seriously wounded him with a double barreled shotgun. The next stage to come along carried Ficklin, who seized the would-be killer, hanged him and calmly rode on. The latter was a mistake, for some friends cut Old Jules down before it was too late. Being convinced that hiding was the better part of valor, the old trader led his crew to the neighborhood of Rocky Ridge, set up headquarters, and committed all kinds of depredations upon the company.

In the meantime Slade, having recovered from his wounds, determined to make an end of the affair. Riding up and down the line he soon located the outlaw hangout. Collecting a party of dependable men, he made a surprise attack in which Old Jules was so badly wounded he could not escape. Slade tied him to a corral post, cut off his ears and nailed them to the fence as a warning to others. When he had done this he fired bullet after bullet into the helpless old villain's body. One of the ears remained there for weeks, it is said, while Slade took the other to wear upon his vest as a watch charm.

About the time the first coaches set out from Leavenworth for Denver, Jones and Russell sent a wagon train loaded with goods for a store to the same place. It arrived early in May. Business was opened in the primitive log cabin at the corner of Blake and F streets formerly occupied by the express company. Since John Armor and H. S. Bulkley were in charge of the office some four months later, it may be assumed that they went out with the train. About a month later another train loaded principally with groceries arrived.

Prior to the founding of the Leavenworth & Pike's Peak Express Company, mail for the Rocky Mountain region was sent over Hockaday & Company's stage line to Fort Laramie, where it was picked up and carried on to its destination. The express company, with its promise of regular service, was regarded almost as a gift from heaven by the isolated, news-hungry gold-seekers. The fee of twenty-five cents for letters, ten cents for newspapers, and one dollar a pound for express packages seemed unbelievably low.

From the day when the first coaches left Denver for Leavenworth, carrying $700 worth of gold, they transported it regularly in varying amounts. To handle these shipments, at a rate based upon their value, four messengers were employed. The first ones were Clay Thompson, George Speer, C. W. Wiley and a man by the name of Filligrew.

In founding the stage line, locating home stations, and opening regular traffic between the Missouri River and the Rocky Mountains, Jones and Russell made an incalculable contribution toward the settlement of the wide plains along the route. As had always been the case with the westward creeping frontier, once reasonably dependable transportation was assured, either overland or by water, the people flocked into the area and established new homes. Settlers followed the coaches and freight wagons out across Kansas, along the Platte River and its South Fork, down to Denver, and from there out into the mountains to scores of towns and ranches. All of them at first depended upon the Leavenworth & Pike's Peak Express Company to keep them in contact with the older sections of the country back East. The proprietors were therefore colonizers although they would have been the last to make that claim for themselves.

VII
R. B. BRADFORD & COMPANY

LTHOUGH Russell's relations with Waddell were severely strained during the spring and summer of 1859 he continued to bend every effort toward promoting the interests of Russell, Majors & Waddell. About the first of March, Quartermaster General Jesup notified Russell that he wished the firm to transport 843,000 pounds of flour to Utah for the use of troops still at Camp Floyd and other places. This request was relayed to Waddell at Leavenworth. Immediately he began buying wagons, oxen, and equipment. Bids for supplying the flour were also called for by the Quartermaster's Department. Among others, Gilbert & Gerrish, Salt Lake City merchants and freighters, responded. Their bid, based wholly upon flour ground in Utah, was thrown aside upon the advice of the Chief Commissary Officer at Camp Floyd, who urged the Department not to depend upon Utah for a pound of flour. The contract was therefore let to mills in St. Louis, Mo.[84]

While these things were happening, Russell closed his business in Washington and went to New York, on his way to Leavenworth. In New York he met his old friend, Ben Holladay. During his business career Holladay had been store clerk, saloon and hotel keeper, postmaster at Weston, Missouri, miller, government contractor, merchant at Salt Lake City, cattle dealer, and a number of other things. In the course of their conversations Holladay, who was far more familiar with Salt Lake Valley resources than Russell himself, assured him that, notwithstanding the advice of the Commissary Officer at Camp Floyd, good flour could be obtained in Utah. Why not take the Quartermaster's contract with the St. Louis mills off his hands and supply Camp Floyd with flour manufactured in Salt Lake Valley? The Missouri product could easily be sold on the market at a handsome profit. This appealed to Russell, for flour could be bought in Utah for about what it cost in St. Louis. The deal was simple, providing the Secretary of War was agreeable to it. After thinking it over Russell said he would undertake it if Holladay would

[84] *Lexington Weekly Express*, Oct. 28, 1859.

become a partner to the contract, go to Utah, and handle the business there. Holladay consented. In Washington, Secretary Floyd readily agreed to the proposition on condition that Russell, Majors & Waddell buy the St. Louis flour and supply any deficiency which might arise because of a shortage in Utah with superfine Missouri product.[85] This was the first business connection between Holladay and the freighting firm over whose destinies he was to exercise a weighty influence within a short time.

Out in Salt Lake Valley, Holladay made contracts for the flour and laid plans for assembling wagons and teams to deliver it. Charles Byers, office manager at Leavenworth, also went out to Utah to help with the work, and Russell expected to buy the flour for less than five dollars per one hundred pounds. During the early part of July, Holladay bought 782 mules, 7 horses, 21 wagons, harness, and other items at auction from the Quartermaster at Camp Floyd. These were for the purpose of delivering the flour for which he had contracted. In payment, he wrote a draft upon Russell for $73,267.50.

Everything went along smoothly with the contract until about the time Holladay bought the equipment at Camp Floyd. Then Horace Greeley, still being "dead-headed" by the Leavenworth & Pike's Peak Express Company, stumped into Salt Lake Valley on his way to California, his tow-colored fringe of hair and old linen duster floating in the mountain breezes. Animated by journalistic curiosity, anti-Administration sentiments, zeal for the still juvenile Republican party, and the true newshawk's instinct for the sensational, he poked around to see what he could find. Upon discovering that Brigham Young was reported to have made $50,000 on the lumber to build barracks at Camp Floyd, his indignation bubbled. "The army does nothing but enrich the contractors favored by the War Department and the saintly speculators of Mormondom," he trumpeted. He also suspected that the Army was kept in Utah solely for the pecuniary gain of those same contractors. Next he turned up Russell and Holladay's flour contract. Knowing that the rate for freighting supplies from the Missouri River was $22.50 per one hundred pounds, he found that by "a little dextrous management at Washington" the flour was bought in Utah for seven cents per pound. Straightway he informed the world that a clear profit of $170,000 had been made on the

[85] J. V. Frederick, *Ben Holladay: The Stagecoach King*, pp. 1, 21, 24, 28, 30, 32, 40, 65. Russell to Waddell, Apr. 29, May 5, 1859. *Lexington Weekly Express*, Oct. 8, 1859.

contract. His article was published in the *New York Tribune* and widely copied in the East.

With the unfavorable publicity the firm was receiving, financing it was no easy task. Regardless of all, however, Russell was as optimistic as usual. Nothing seemed to discourage him for any length of time. Waddell's dissatisfaction with him for having organized the express company and constant complaints at length caused Russell to regret that he had gone into the company at all. On July 5, 1859, he wrote that he would get out of it when he came home, which would be soon. He accomplished this the latter part of the year, but not in the manner implied in his letter.

Although relations between Russell and Waddell were not good in the spring and summer of 1859 and the financial outlook threatening, the three partners got together to launch a new enterprise. Majors and Waddell had made up their minds that there really was something to that "Pike's Peak" business after all. Consequently, they formed a partnership with Robert B. Bradford of Lexington, a relative of Waddell, to ship a wagon-train load of goods to Denver and open a store under the name of R. B. Bradford & Company.[86] Bradford was to go out and operate it, receiving one third of the profits as remuneration. The goods were to be furnished by Russell, Majors & Waddell at Leavenworth cost, plus ten cents per pound for freight across the plains.

By September 22, Bradford had reached Denver, having passed the train on the way. Another was to come later in the fall. Some of the flour taken off the Quartermaster's hands was probably in those wagons. He bought a lot at the corner of Blake and G streets and began the erection of a two-story wooden building, sixty feet long and fifty feet wide. While it was being built he bought and occupied the log shanty that the express company and Jones, Russell & Company's store had occupied.[87] Since the business was booming he opened some of his goods and displayed them for sale. On October 13 an advertisement in the *Rocky Mountain News* offered clothing by the package, i.e., at wholesale.

Bradford was delighted with the prospects offered by the new country. On September 23 he cautiously wrote Waddell that he was much encouraged by the great success of the miners in the various diggings.

[86] Contract between Russell, Majors & Waddell and R. B. Bradford, Aug. 3, 1859.
[87] Bradford to Waddell, Sept. 22. Oct. 19, 1859. *Colorado Magazine*, VIII, 168.

Good businessman that he was, he had come out with an open mind and was not inclined to snap judgments. He warned Waddell not to expect too great a volume of business that fall because they were late in appearing upon the scene. The stampede of immigrants was over.

From the very beginning Bradford saw that the Leavenworth & Pike's Peak Express Company was doomed to failure. He felt there had been recklessness and waste in setting it up and prophesied that when a true inventory was made it would "foot up ugly." The Jones, Russell & Company store, however, was doing very well with sales averaging $250 per day. At that time Bradford was cannily coasting along, selling a few goods for a small profit, waiting for his store building to be completed. A little later on he would have the only complete stock of goods in Denver. By this time he had formed his opinion of "Pike's Peak." "Unless every indication a business man can ask for should fail," he wrote Waddell, "I see nothing to prevent us from doing a business next spring that will be of a magnitude to satisfy even R. M. W." [88]

Bradford looked this newest of frontiers over with the eye of an experienced businessman and inaugurated a program of speculative activities not unlike that of his three partners. The town of St. Vrain, a day's travel from Denver, appeared such a strong rival for the honor of being the metropolis of the Rockies that he bought five hundred shares in it. Within two or three years, he thought, Denver or St. Vrain would be twice the size of Leavenworth. By the end of the year he also owned forty shares in the town of Breckinridge, five lots to the share, and an interest in another town, called Bradford in honor of himself. At the edge of this town he took up a claim for Waddell, upon which the shareholders suggested that a palace of "marble and granite" be built to accommodate the owner when he came west, which he did not do until 1864. Bradford helped to organize a company to build a toll road running from Denver to the town of Bradford, via the present Littleton, to be known as the Bradford Road, and he planned to erect store buildings at that place and Breckinridge. In partnership with Amos Steck, successor to Henry Fields as postmaster for the Leavenworth & Pike's Peak Express Company, he got hold of a "coal bank" and an iron mine. Together with Steck, Jones, Cartright, and six others, Bradford organized the Denver Mutual Fire Insurance Company and got a charter from the legislature of the Terri-

[88] Bradford to Waddell, Sept, 22, Oct. 19, 1859.

tory of Jefferson on December 7, 1859. It was capitalized at $50,000, which could be increased to $500,000.[89]

In 1860 he bought a ranch in partnership with W. H. Middaugh, where he grazed Russell, Majors & Waddell's cattle and grew turnips and potatoes for the market. During the preceding winter he had helped organize the Capital Hydraulic Ditch Company, which was incorporated by the Kansas Territorial Legislature. It was capitalized for $500,000, had sixteen stockholders, including himself and Waddell. They planned for it to extend from Denver to the canyon of the Platte, nine miles away. In the midsummer of 1860, Bradford expressed confidence that its income, once in operation, would be so fabulous that neither of them would be compelled to "work for bread and meat" in their old age. At that time the Bradford Road was paying well, and he thought it would average $500 per week in 1861. Meanwhile, some friends discovered what they thought was a silver mine in the mountains and enrolled Bradford as an original shareholder. About the same time he said that if he were free from the store he could make $10,000 on the investments he had made for himself and Waddell.[90]

From the very beginning R. B. Bradford & Company was a highly important cog in the affairs of Russell, Majors & Waddell in Denver, although technically it was entirely separate and apart from it. Since there was no one else in the city to look after the latter firm's interests, Bradford was commissioned to do so. There was talk of moving its store from Fort Laramie down to Denver, and Waddell spoke of sending surplus wagons and oxen from the Missouri River for sale there. With unerring insight Bradford saw the complications which would inevitably arise from the fact that John S. Jones was a partner in the express company, Cartright & Jones, and Jones, Russell & Company. Almost from the first day of Bradford's residence in Denver, he urged Russell, Majors & Waddell to buy the two stores and the express company's interest in the Denver City Town Company, providing they could be bought for $500 to $700 per share. When the deal transferring the Leavenworth & Pike's Peak Express Company and the Jones, Russell & Company's store to Russell, Majors & Waddell was made, he renewed his plea that Cartright

[89] Bradford to Waddell, Oct. 19, Nov. 3, Dec. 15, 1859, Jan. 13, 18, 1860. *Colorado Magazine*, IX, 66, 67, 145.

[90] Bradford to Waddell, Sept. 22, Oct. 19, Nov. 3, Dec. 15, 1859, Mar. 8, May 1, June 5, July 18, Aug. 13-25, 1860. Bradford, Petition to Supreme Court, Sept. 28, 1861.

Advertisements from
the *Leavenworth City
Directory*, 1859–60

& Jones be bought out also. Such a transaction, he said, would give R. B. Bradford & Company control of the flour market until trains could arrive from New Mexico in the spring. By December 1, 1860, he was urging Waddell either to buy Ceran St. Vrain's mill in that Territory or make some kind of arrangements with him so that they might control that market.[91]

Unfortunately both Russell and Waddell failed to catch the full significance of what was happening in the "Pike's Peak" region and heavily discounted Bradford's burning enthusiasm. They denounced his private speculations, accused him of neglecting the business of R. B. Bradford & Company, and refused to give him power of attorney that he might protect the express company's town lots. They complained that his remittances of cash and gold dust were too meager, insinuated that he spent his time playing billiards and gambling, and accepted as true, vicious gossip concerning him and a young-woman school teacher who went to Denver from Lexington. By early 1860, Russell and Majors were "down" on him and undertook to deal with him as though he were a mere agent instead of a partner. He angrily wrote Waddell:

You, nor Russell, nor Majors have ever seen the day when you could rank me in position, family, or character, and if you do not hold me in that place it will become my duty to make it appear . . . . Be assured that the good or bad opinion of Messrs Russell and Majors will have no effect on me, unless it is based on facts. I am not so poor as to become the recipient of their favors unless I do so on an equality with either of them . . . . Tell them to come and relieve me. I owe them nothing but kindness so far, but if they undertake to discuss my conduct or my character, let them do it as becomes men, and allow me the privilege of defending myself . . . . While I will cheerfully obey instructions I will not consent to be dictated to in terms unbecoming a man or gentleman.[92]

After a few acrimonious letters in which each spoke his mind, this flurry blew over and matters moved along smoothly. Bradford came off rather well in these long range verbal fisticuffs. He stood firmly upon his rights and dignity and bluntly informed Waddell that if they were not satisfied with what he was doing to send someone out to take his place.

[91] Bradford to Waddell, Sept. 13, 22, Oct. 13, 19, Nov. 3, 21, 29, Dec. 15, 1859.
[92] Bradford to Waddell, Jan. 5, Feb. 2, 3, July 4, 20, 1860. Russell to Waddell, Nov. 22, 28, 1859.

The store buildings he mentioned were erected and improvements made upon property belonging to himself and Waddell.

In April 1860, Bradford went back to Leavenworth and Lexington for a fortnight, but the visit with Waddell did not improve their relations. On May 1, the Central Overland California & Pike's Peak Express Company having been organized, he turned the express business over to J. B. Jones. When the work of getting that organization into operation was finished, hard feelings arose again between Bradford and Waddell. In mid-June he delivered another ultimatum.

You are evidently becoming quite uneasy about our business here, and as I do not intend to quarrel with you any more or even exchange unkind words it would probably be better to close at the earliest possible period . . . . There is no necessity for any language to pass between us, other than that of business and kindly feelings. You seem to listen to many things said about my poor self, and upon the strength of said *gossip* immediately take me to task as though it were true. This I cannot help, of course, but does it not seem very strange to you that nobody ever speaks well of me? [93]

This outburst cleared the atmosphere again and peace reigned for a time.

In addition to all other burdens imposed by circumstances upon a pioneer business man, Bradford was compelled to furnish supplies to the Central Overland California & Pike's Peak Express Company, and to Alexander Majors, and cash drafts for both. By the middle of March 1860, the express company owed R. B. Bradford & Company $20,000, which, by the latter part of May, had been reduced to $12,384.42. In July, Bradford was paying out $500 to $1,200 per week for the two. Sums paid to Majors were charged to his personal account but those to the express company were charged to Russell, Majors & Waddell. After a stormy career of about fourteen months the dissolution of R. B. Bradford & Company was announced in November, 1860.[94] The creeping blight of the Civil War, the deteriorating fortunes of Russell, Majors & Waddell, and unfavorable business conditions in the Rocky Mountain region made this necessary.

On January 8, 1861, he wrote Waddell that he had sold the stock of goods and the building housing it to Alexander Majors, who bought it

[93] Bradford to Waddell, Dec. 22, 1859, Feb. 23, May 1, Mar. 15, June 14, 1860.
[94] Bradford to Waddell, Mar. 15, 1860.

for Russell, Majors & Waddell. This, he thought, would solve his problems and relieve him of a partnership which had been exceedingly disappointing. When an inventory was taken it was found that the purchase price was about $40,000. From this amount a bill for $3,140 that Bradford owed Russell, Majors & Waddell was to be deducted and the remainder paid to Waddell at Leavenworth or Lexington. Before this could be carried out the news of Russell's trouble over the abstracted bonds in Washington arose. Waddell hurried to Independence for a conference with Alexander Majors, who was sick in bed. On January 22, Waddell wrote Bradford that the sale of the stock of goods and building should be annulled immediately because he was making assignment of all his property to trustees for the benefit of creditors. To William S. Hays, agent for Russell, Majors & Waddell in Denver, he also wrote instructions to return the goods and building to Bradford. This was signed "Russell, Majors & Waddell," by W. B. Waddell.[95]

In another and more personal letter to Hays, on the same date, Waddell said,

> We are compelled on acct of Russell's difficulties to make assignment of all their own property of R. M. W. for the benefit of endorsees. Therefore if Bradford's goods is not returned to him at once he will lose their value. You might still stay in the house until you sell out. In a few days we shall send our agent to receive all the property of R. M. W. and place it in your charge. Majors is here sick or we should have met at Leavenworth. All hands and employees are well protected and will be paid. . . . . Keep these remarks quiet.

Three days later another letter signed by both Waddell and Majors was forwarded to Hays. This one instructed him to take fourteen hundred sacks of flour from the R. B. Bradford & Company store, sell it, and forward the amount received, $14,087.50, to four individuals, one of whom was Waddell's son, John W. The remainder of the property, they said, had been assigned to Alexander W. Street, Eugene B. Allen, and Francis G. Ewing, as trustees for the benefit of endorsees. Bradford agreed to these arrangements with the understanding that Hays, as agent for the assignees should, out of the first money coming in for the sale of goods, pay him $18,800 which was due him from the store. Hays proceeded to sell the goods, but instead of paying Bradford forwarded the

95 Waddell to Hays, Jan. 22, 1860.

money to the trustees. On July 10, 1861, Bradford had a conference in Leavenworth with the members of the freighting firm and Eugene B. Allen. They agreed that Bradford should return to Denver and Hays would pay him, but payment was not made. In September, Bradford sued Russell, Majors & Waddell, the trustees, and Hays in the Colorado courts.[96] So ended the career of R. B. Bradford & Company.

[96] Bradford, Petition to Supreme Court, Sept. 28, 1861.

VIII

CENTRAL OVERLAND CALIFORNIA & PIKE'S PEAK EXPRESS COMPANY

VERYBODY'S PROPHECIES of disaster for the Leavenworth & Pike's Peak Express Company came true. It lost money from the day of its beginning. Waddell and Majors watched it with heavy forebodings. In fact, these conservative partners of Russell saw clearly that if the express company went by the board it might take Russell, Majors & Waddell with it.

By the middle of October 1859, Waddell was alarmed over the situation and saw that something had to be done. Bradford advised him to take the express company over and, if Russell, Majors & Waddell did not get the freighting contract for 1860-61, to concentrate everything in Denver and Colorado. With the approach of November the sands ran out for the express company. The concern owed $525,532 by that time. Among the items was $190,269 owed to Russell, Majors & Waddell; $116,807 on other accounts; $10,000 to employees, and $23,000 to John S. Jones. Among its assets was $18,250 received for 400 mules sold by W. B. Waddell at Lexington and Miami, Missouri; the stock of goods in the Jones, Russell & Company store in Denver, $30,800; 543 mules, $60,890; 125 wagons, $10,000; 60 coaches, $15,000; on invoice of Hockaday & Company's coaches and stations, $90,000; mail pay on the Hockaday & Company contract to November 15, 1860, $198,750. These items made up a total of $423,690. Other smaller ones brought the total to $525,532.[97]

On October 28, 1859, Russell, Majors & Waddell took over the bankrupt concern under a contract which provided for the formation of a new company for the purpose of transporting freight and carrying United States mail and passengers. The capital stock was fixed at $200,000 and divided into forty shares. The shareholders in it and the number of shares they held were as follows: William B. Waddell, 2; Alexander Majors, 2; John W. Russell, 2; John S. Jones, 4; William H. Russell, 30.

[97] Bradford to Waddell, Oct. 19, 1859. Jones, Russell & Co., Balance Sheet, Nov. 18, 1859.

They gave Russell power of attorney and proxies and authorized him to associate other persons with them by the sale of stock. John S. Jones was elected superintendent and John W. Russell secretary, with salaries of $3,000 and $1,800 per year respectively.[98] There the matter rested for a few months. In the meantime the concern continued to operate under the name of Leavenworth & Pike's Peak Express Company as though nothing had happened.

When the trains laden with army supplies reached Camp Floyd late in the summer of 1859, Dr. J. Hobbs, agent for Russell, Majors & Waddell at that place, selected 3,500 head of the best oxen to send to California the following spring. Since these animals were at a premium in that new country, the owners thought it would be more profitable to sell them on the Pacific coast than to drive them back to the Missouri River. The wagons brought out were probably used by Holladay in delivering flour to Camp Floyd and other places. About September 20 the oxen left Camp Floyd in charge of Jackson Cooper and a man by the name of Oldham, bound for Ruby Valley, a grassy mountain nook some three hundred miles away in the northeast corner of the present state of Nevada. On the way the men found little grass for the animals, and they passed numerous parties of stranded, suffering immigrants who were traveling behind schedule. While yet three days from their destination a heavy snowstorm howled down upon them. They reached Ruby Valley, but found from two and a half to three feet of snow upon the ground. The weather continued bad, and up to January 1, 1861, they had scarcely seen the sun. The wind blew furiously and the snow drifted so deep that it was impossible to drive the oxen to the sides of the mountains where shelter and a bit of grass was available. By January 6, fifteen hundred of them had died and when spring came only two hundred remained alive. This loss was estimated at $150,000.[99]

In the latter part of 1859, Russell, his partners, and his friends in Washington began to fear that the freighting monopoly might not be renewed for another two-year period. There was good reason for this fear. The Administration, the War Department, and the contractors themselves were under heavy attack. In August the Bank of America in

[98] Contract between Russell, Majors & Waddell and John S. Jones, *et al.*, Oct. 28, 1859. Rufus Sage, *Out of the West*, p. 166.

[99] Jackson Cooper to Waddell, Jan. 6, 1860. A. B. Miller to Waddell, Mar. 1, 1860.

New York protested $25,000 worth of acceptances which had been sold to the Merchants Bank of St. Louis, Mo. Russell declared this action unjust and unnecessary, but the news went abroad in financial circles anyway. This, together with freely expressed doubts as to the legality of the acceptances, made it difficult for James T. Soutter, president of the Bank of the Republic in New York and Russell's loyal friend, to negotiate them. The result was a heavy overdraft at that bank in the latter part of August for which Soutter provided.

In spite of shoals, reefs, and gathering clouds, Russell was as sanguine as ever. "If we can manage Dec.," he wrote on November 22, 1859, "I have no fears. That we must and will. I will not give up so long as a two inch plank remains on the deck of our schooner. Think we can anchor her and no mistake."

In the same letter he expressed perfect confidence in the future of the new express company and said he had sold shares in it to Jerome B. Simpson. He disclosed its name for the first time, the Central Overland California & Pike's Peak Express Company. At this time he also felt that their investments in Denver would turn out all right. In fact he was certain his one share in the Denver City Town Company, which only cost him $250.00, would yield him "a handsome house." His feelings on that day were clearly and briefly expressed when he said, "I am much rejoiced at your report from Pike's Peak." Six days later his optimism had oozed away and things looked black again. "I fear next month," he confessed, "indeed I do not see how we can get through with it if the flour receipts do not come in soon, which I much fear." On December 21 he wrote Waddell that he had arranged with Soutter to discount $150,000 worth of acceptances, for which the latter was liberally paid. He had also written Samuel & Allen in St. Louis to discount them at any rate they could. "We must now go through," he declared, "cannot think of aught else." They did go "through" but the margin was exceedingly narrow.

Some time in the latter part of the year someone made up a financial statement which indicated that the assets of the partners amounted to $1,510,000.[100] This included the Russell & Waddell interests, beef cattle, flour on hand, Miller, Russell & Company, the Central Overland Cali-

---

[100] Russell, Majors & Waddell, Statement of Assets (n.d.).

fornia & Pike's Peak Express Company, R. B. Bradford & Company, oxen at Leavenworth and in Utah, wagons, bills of lading, merchandise, and real estate. About the same time a statement of liabilities showed bills falling due in December 1859, to the amount of $250,000. The story of obligations due in that month was only the beginning. A schedule showing those falling due the first six months of 1860 was as follows:

December 1859	$ 250,000.00
January	217,923.87
February	213,355.12
March	240,930.00
April	45,937.61
May	6,390,25
June	26,652.87
Total	$1,001,189.72

Of that amount $300,000 was for acceptances payable in January, February, and March, 1860. They owed banks for loans and discounted acceptances, individuals for the same, wholesalers, and employees for their services. The difference between the book value of assets and liabilities was $418,809.48. Losses of cattle in Ruby Valley had not yet been reported when these statements were made up. These alone reduced the book value of their balance to $268,809.48, granting that this sum represented actual value, which it did not.

The exact truth was that Russell, Majors & Waddell was bankrupt by the close of the year 1859. Waddell and Majors knew it, others suspected it, but Russell would not—dared not—admit it. The very situation seemed to inflame his imagination and prompt him to soar off into new speculations. While in this mood he remembered some things Robert B. Bradford had said in his enthusiastic letters concerning Denver and the Rocky Mountain region. "I feel inclined," said he, "to agree with Bradford that that is the place to make our money instead of freighting." [101] That was what Bradford had been telling Waddell for a long time. Unfortunately, until now Russell had been too busy even to answer most of Bradford's letters. With disaster in clear view upon the horizon he began to cast about for a safe haven.

[101] Russell to Waddell, Aug. 30, Nov. 22, Dec. 30, 1859, Jan. 3, May 11, 1860.

CALIFORNIA & PIKE'S PEAK EXPRESS

With characteristic, annoying brevity, Alexander Majors said that Russell, Majors & Waddell took over the inflated Leavenworth & Pike's Peak Express Company and paid its debts to save their partner and protect money advanced to it. This transaction was a plain, everyday business imperative to avoid going under in the latter part of 1859. The impairment of Russell's credit and standing would certainly have caused a collapse of the now wobbly freighting firm. But saving Russell's face and protecting loans amounting to $50,000 was not all there was to it. Not by any means. Had the firm been in good condition and this their only object they could have sold the Hockaday & Company contract and line, disposed of the defunct express company's equipment, charged the whole affair to experience, profit and loss, and gone ahead. They did not do this. The contract by which they took it over provided for complete reorganization. Not only that, but they went immediately to work improving the lines and service between Denver and Salt Lake City.

Regardless of the implication that the Leavenworth & Pike's Peak Express Company was taken in as a kind of doorstep baby, there is much to indicate that its adoption was not unwelcome. Through the Hockaday & Company contract they had at last gotten into the business of carrying the United States mail on the Central Route. The contract by which they took the express company over clearly reveals their intentions. It says the purpose was "to organize a company by incorporation or otherwise for the purpose of carrying, conveying, or transporting goods, wares, or merchandise, also passengers to Pike's Peak or elsewhere and to carry mail to and from Utah or to and from any other point." They had a mail contract on the Central Route, extending halfway across the Continent, possessed the equipment for carrying mail, express, freight, and passengers; and prospects looked good.

When Russell returned to New York in the fall of 1859, after taking over the Leavenworth & Pike's Peak Express Company and setting up the new organization, his partners thought he would work to interest new capital in the latter concern, but he did not. Instead, he admitted only Jerome B. Simpson, on some terms other than cash, and he said that, if they could get along with only the $50,000 to $100,000 that additional stockholders would bring in, they could get along without it. In December, 1859, he sent J. B. Jones, an old California miner, to Denver to study the situation and make reports. With the assistance of Robert B.

Bradford, Jones analyzed business conditions in that city, visited the diggings in the mountains, and returned to New York the latter part of January with glowing reports. On his way he stopped at Leavenworth and at Lexington, where he talked with Waddell and possibly with Majors.[102]

While Jones was on his tour, Russell organized the Central Overland California & Pike's Peak Express Company in New York and got up a charter for presentation to the Kansas Territorial Legislature. The incorporators were William H. Russell, John S. Jones, Benjamin Ficklin, Alexander Majors, Benjamin C. Card, Webster M. Samuel, Jerome B. Simpson, William B. Waddell, William S. Grant, Luther R. Smoot, and Joseph A. Monheimer. The capital stock was $500,000, divided into shares of $100 each, which might be increased by a two-thirds vote of the majority of stockholders. The charter gave the company the right to operate express, stage, passenger, and transportation routes by land or water, for the conveyance of persons, mail, or property in Kansas or beyond its limits. In addition the company had the right to write fire and marine insurance, to explore for minerals and operate mines and assaying plants, to write life insurance or annuities, and to receive money in trust. It was organized November 23, 1859, with William H. Russell as president and his son John W. as secretary.[103]

By December 1 all the stock had been subscribed. The people of Leavenworth regarded the charter as "the great bill" of the session and the Leavenworth *Times* envisioned the city as "in a nearly straight line from the cities of the East to the gold fields of the West." The enterprise, it said, "was one of mammoth character" and would "play a great part in the rapid development of the vast region between the Missouri and the Pacific . . . . and will make the line of the Pacific Railroad."

Late in 1859 Russell was certain the firm would again secure a two-year monopoly upon the freighting of government supplies to Utah and other places in the West for 1860-61. The army at Camp Floyd was being reduced, but he expected to use one thousand wagons anyway. His hopes were still high the first week in January, but he began to talk a new language—economy. This must have pleased Waddell greatly. All sur-

---

[102] Russell to Waddell, Nov. 22, 1859. Bradford to Waddell, Jan. 5, 18, 25, 26, 1860.

[103] *Act to Incorporate the Central Overland California & Pike's Peak Express Company*, 1860. *Laws of Kansas Territory*, 1859, pp. 254-259. *Federal Cases*, Book 21, pp. 306-312. Russell to Waddell, Dec. 19, 1860.

plus oxen and equipment were to be sold and nothing which did not pay expenses was to be kept going. He felt that Congress would act favorably upon their claim for losses in Utah in 1857 and that all would go well until March, 1861. After that he made no promises. All resources, he insisted, had to be utilized in the payment of debts. Moreover, he was confident that a contract to supply four or five thousand head of beef cattle for the troops in Utah and Arizona undoubtedly would be given them.

On April 11, 1860, another contract for a two-year period, 1860-61, was signed with Captain Stewart Van Vliet, Assistant Quartermaster at Fort Leavenworth.[104] This time it covered only the New Mexico posts. Supplies to be transported over the Oregon Trail to Utah went to others. The reason for this new arrangement is obscure. It may have been that pressure upon the Administration and the War Department finally broke the monopoly Russell and his partners had held since 1855. Or it could have been that Russell, Majors & Waddell, owing to acute financial difficulties, were unable to outfit themselves as in the past. Whatever the reason, the loss of the monopoly served to weaken their already precarious position.

With the signing of this contract, Leavenworth as a starting point for trains destined for New Mexico and the Southwest was practically abandoned. Kansas City now became the principal starting point for trains billed to that section of the country. Great stone warehouses were built on the levee and fifteen hundred wagons were shipped in on steamboats and parked in the bottom along the bluffs. Four thousand cattle and 140 mules were also brought in. The finest and most commodious business house in the place, consisting of two rooms forty by one hundred feet, was opened to receive goods for outfitting the men in the employ of Russell, Majors & Waddell. In the latter part of May, Alexander Majors called a meeting of his bullwhackers in one of the warehouses. After reading the First Psalm he talked for two hours on the various aspects of clean moral living. During his ten years of freighting, he said, he had made the Bible his rule of action. If his hearers would study and follow it they would succeed in life. He disclaimed being an educated man, but declared he had sense enough to know right from wrong. In conclusion

---

104 Contract between Russell, Majors & Waddell and Captain Stewart Van Vliet, April 11, 1860.

he hoped the bullwhackers would think about what he said and try to be upright, moral men.

Up to September 20, 1860, they had sent out 837 wagons, carrying 5,007,686 pounds of freight. In addition to those belonging to the firm, Majors had 500 wagons and 2140 mules in the Pike's Peak trade. These were his own private property and had no connection with Russell, Majors & Waddell whatever. He also owned an outfitting store in Kansas City on Main Street between Second and Third streets.[105]

[105] *Kansas City Directory*, 1860-61, pp. 17, 85.

IX

MAIL TO CALIFORNIA

HEN the United States annexed California and adja-
cent territory at the close of the War with Mexico,
the question of the best land route thither began to
be debated. Where the route to California was concerned the immigrants settled the matter for themselves by following
the old Oregon trail, at first by way of Fort Hall and the Humboldt
River to Sacramento. The road through Salt Lake City was merely a
variation in the interests of economy in time and space. The major portion of gold seekers traveling overland chose the Central Route. Had
there been no question at issue save the shortest and most comfortable
road to California, that route would have easily prevailed over all others.
Unfortunately, there was much more in it than a friendly argument over
the best road from one point in the country to another.

That something else was the fascinating, stupendous project of a
railroad from the Mississippi River to the Pacific coast. The annexation
of California gave impetus to the idea. As early as 1834 the East was in
a ferment of railroad building. In that year the legislature of New York
chartered ten companies. In 1837 Dr. Hartwell Carver of the *New York
Courier and Inquirer* ballyhooed a road stretching from the Mississippi
River to the Pacific, providing the Rocky Mountains, about which people knew very little, could be crossed. If that were impossible, he advo-
cated building it to the head of navigation on the Columbia River. As
usual where men of broad, accurate vision are concerned, the indifferent
and ignorant undertook to smother him under an avalanche of ridicule.
With true prophetic toughness he clung to his idea and went to Washington, hoping to interest Congress in his scheme. There he found another man of vision, Asa Whitney, a New York merchant who traded
with China.[106]

On January 28, 1845, Whitney presented a memorial to Congress
asking that a strip of land sixty miles wide, extending from Lake Michi-

[106] *Kansas Historical Quarterly,* XI, 529-532.

gan to the Pacific Coast be conveyed to him and his heirs on condition that they build a track through it. It was his intention that immigrants and homesteaders should do the work and pay for land with their wages. The road was to belong to the public, tolls being charged for its operation. He wrote a book on the subject, traveled extensively in the United States in behalf of it, and explored eight hundred miles of the route. Twenty state legislatures and various city councils endorsed his plan. In 1852 the House of Representatives in Washington reported favorably upon it and suggested that the strip of land, some 78,000,000 acres of "good, bad, and indifferent" soil be sold to him at ten cents per acre and paid for when the road was completed.

Next in line of prophetic succession was William Gilpin, West Pointer, Mexican War veteran, promoter of the dream city of Centropolis at the mouth of the Kansas River, and later first Territorial Governor of Colorado. He, too, wrote a book, lectured whenever and wherever anybody would listen, and urged Congress to do something about a railroad to the Pacific. Contemporaneous with both Whitney and Gilpin was Senator Thomas Hart Benton of Missouri, "Father of the West." In the late 1820's he succeeded in getting an appropriation from Congress for the surveying and marking of the Santa Fe trail from the Missouri River to Santa Fe, New Mexico. Although he was opposed to Whitney's magnificent scheme, he was in favor of a transcontinental railroad. In 1849 he introduced a bill in the Senate providing for the construction of a railroad from St. Louis to the Pacific. Work was begun in midsummer, 1851, and the road reached Jefferson City in 1855.

It is significant that early advocates of a transcontinental railroad were, with the exception of Benton and Gilpin, residents of the East whose sole motive was the development of agriculture, commerce, and transportation. Had the matter of choosing the route been left to men of unprejudiced business judgment, and had the decision been based entirely upon geographical considerations, there is no question about which would have been chosen. The Central Route would have easily carried away all honors. Unfortunately for the nation and Russell, Majors & Waddell, the decision did not rest with men of that type.

To fully understand the fierce contest over the route to the Pacific, one must revert to the beginning of our national history. The Constitution was, in some very important provisions, wholly the result of compromise between the northern and southern sections of the nation. Harmony between the two prevailed until new lands in Northwest Territory were opened for settlement. The Ordinances set up to govern them in 1787 were born in the wedlock of compromise. So long as the western boundary of the United States was the Mississippi River, relations between North and South were reasonably harmonious. The Louisiana Purchase of 1804 automatically raised the old issue regarding free and slave territory and the Missouri Compromise of 1820 was the result. By this device the South maintained its balance of power in the Senate and the future again seemed reassuring.

With the acquisition of territory from Mexico in 1848, the thorn in the flesh of the body politic began to cause trouble again. The crisis confronting the South and its slave institution was obvious. Southern politicians looked at maps, studied reports of travelers west of the Mississippi River, and girded themselves for a final, conclusive battle. A vast, unsettled territory, much of it entirely unsuited to slave labor, might be colonized by people of anti-slavery sentiments and organized into free states. Should that happen, the rigidly maintained balance of power in the Senate would be destroyed and the pre-eminence of the South in Congress brought to an end.

Politicians, as well as everybody else, knew that whichever section of the country controlled the Pacific railroad would possess a tremendous advantage over the other. They also knew that, nature being allowed to take its course, the railroad would follow one of the main immigration routes. In 1855 the War Department mapped five possible ones but everybody knew that no more than three, at best, would ever be given serious consideration. These were the Northern, Central, and Southern.

The controversy over these routes involved not only a transcontinental railroad, but also, after the settlement of California, an overland mail from the Missouri River. In fact, the latter temporarily pushed the former into the background from the early 1850's to the opening of the Civil War. Naturally, the people of both the Pacific Coast and Missouri exhibited a deep interest in the matter of communication between the two widely separated portions of the country. Out in California this interest was expressed in a two-volume memorial calling for a good wagon road and an overland mail, which was sent to Congress in 1856. The interest of Missourians in the matter induced the state legislature to charter the Missouri & California Overland Mail and Transportation Company in 1855. A capital stock of three million dollars was authorized and the issue of bonds permitted. Among the incorporators who were to choose a board of directors were many of the most noted men of the state and the West, such as John C. Fremont, Robert Campbell, Francis P. Blair Jr., Samuel H. Woodson, David Waldo, Benjamin Holladay, Robert M. Stewart, James S. Rollins, Ceran St. Vrain, William Gilpin, Albert G. Boone, Charles E. Kearney, Thomas Johnson, Theodore F. Warner, and J. V. T. Thompson. William Gilpin wrote a memorial to Congress asking for a right of way, land grants, and a contract for carrying the mail.[107] While nothing apparently came of this, it is indicative of the widespread concern for communication with California.

Bills authorizing an overland mail were introduced in Congress in 1855 and 1856, but they did not pass. On March 3, 1857, the Post Office Appropriation Bill, which bore an amendment authorizing an overland mail to California, became law. It provided $300,000 for a semimonthly service, or $450,000 for a weekly service, or $600,000 for a semiweekly service. The service was to be performed with good four-horse coaches or spring wagons suitable for carrying both passengers and mail. It was expected that stations would be built along the way and 320 acres of land were to be given where each was located. The time was to be twenty-five days each way. No route having been named in the bill, the responsibility for choosing one fell upon the Postmaster General.[108]

Among the bidders was John Butterfield, who acted for Butterfield & Company. Back of this firm was an interesting chapter in the history of the development of express companies in both the East and the West. In the matter of transportation between California and the East, the country had been very much at the mercy of a steamship monopoly which also carried the ocean mail. The victory of the advocates of an overland mail to the Pacific Coast, as represented by the passage of the Post Office Appropriation Bill and its amendments in 1857, appeared to offer an opportunity for the express companies not only to rid themselves of the obnoxious steamship monopoly but also to enter the business of carrying the overland mail. Therefore the great companies, Adams, American,

107 Missouri & California Overland Mail & Transportation Company, 1856. Leroy Hafen, *The Overland Mail*, pp. 83-84.
108 Hafen, pp. 83-88.

National, and Wells, Fargo & Company pooled their interests to form Butterfield & Company, or, as more commonly known, the Overland Mail Company, which was composed of seven men representing them. They were: Butterfield and Alexander Holland for the American; William B. Dinsmore, president of the Adams, William T. Fargo for Wells, Fargo & Company; and James Gardner, Marcus L. Kenyon, and Hamilton Spencer.[109]

Nine bids for carrying the overland mail were received, each designating a starting point on the Mississippi River and the approximate route. Butterfield chose the Southern Route, with St. Louis and Memphis as the points of departure, converging at some place east of Albuquerque, New Mexico. Postmaster General Aaron V. Brown, a Tennesseean, was strongly prejudiced in favor of the route Butterfield named. On September 16, 1857, he awarded the contract to the Overland Mail Company for six years, on the basis of a semiweekly mail at $600,000 per year. The route he designated was from Memphis to St. Louis, converging at Little Rock, Arkansas, and thence via Preston, Texas, and Forts Fillmore and Yuma, to San Diego and San Francisco. As laid down, it was 2800 miles long, in the form of a flat semicircle, and was popularly known in the East as the "Horse-shoe" or "Ox-bow" route. The time was twenty-five days each way. At first the line was equipped with Concord spring wagons but later coaches were added. Stations were built every ten to twenty-five miles.[110]

The line was gotten ready within the required time and service began September 5, 1858. The coaches ran regularly the year round and not too great difficulties with Indians were encountered. The line rendered good service on a reasonably well kept schedule. Northern interests, anti-Administration newspapers, and friends of the Central Route, however, maintained an uproar of criticism and ridicule. Since they could find no fault with the efficiency of the service, their main complaint was against distance and time consumed. In reply, friends of the Southern Route, and even Butterfield himself, admitted that the Central Route was shorter but argued that it could not be traveled in the winter time.

From 1847 to 1850, mail communication between Salt Lake Valley and the outside world was by private, more or less haphazard, methods.

[109] Alvin F. Harlow, *Old Waybills,* p. 203.
[110] Hafen, pp. 89-90.

During those years, there appears to have been no regular, dependable service. The Mormons were too few, too busy establishing themselves in their new home in the wilderness, and above all too poor to think of going to the heavy expense of establishing adequate mail communication with the Missouri River. The Government and people back East took no interest in the matter. For about two years eastbound mail was committed to some trustworthy person who was probably making the journey across the plains for some other reason, and any westbound mail was picked up at Council Bluffs, St. Joseph, or Independence under the same arrangement. Until 1849 the town of Salt Lake City was not even on the maps of the Post Office Department.[111]

In that year the Postmaster General established a post office there, appointed Bishop Joseph L. Heywood postmaster, and authorized a bimonthly mail to Council Bluffs and back. This ran over the old emigration route or Mormon Trail. Almond W. Babbitt took over the responsibility of carrying it at his own expense, receiving the fees in return.[112] He set out from Salt Lake City late in July, 1849, with one man, seven horses, and a light wagon, and arrived at Kanesville, Iowa, on September 3. This arrangement proving unsatisfactory for some reason, it was determined that Allen Compton should take it over. The new service was no more satisfactory than the other, probably because there was too little profit in the work. From the first day of settlement in Salt Lake Valley, inside pressure among Mormons for regular means of communication with the East and the world was very great. The very nature of things made it inevitable. The pioneers of 1847, most of whom were Americans, wanted to maintain contact with relatives and friends back home. And what was equally important, the church had perfected a worldwide organization and had missionaries not only in the States but also in Europe. Contact with them had to be maintained. As a result of their work a stream of immigrants poured across the Plains at almost all seasons of the year, all of whom wished to keep in touch with that part of the world from whence they came.

The first attempt on the part of the government to satisfy this reasonable desire was made early in 1850 when a four-year contract for carrying a monthly mail between Independence, Missouri, and Salt Lake

[111] Hafen, *op. cit.*, pp. 56-57.
[112] Nebraska State Historical Society, *Publications*, XX, 207.

City was let to Samuel H. Woodson of the former place. Service began July 1, 1850, the pay was $19,500 per year and the time thirty days. The route was along the Oregon Trail, past Forts Kearny and Laramie, through South Pass, via Fort Bridger, to its western end. No stations were provided at first and the same teams or set of pack animals made the entire round trip. This arrangement proved more satisfactory than had the others, although many difficulties were encountered which resulted in the mail arriving at both terminals off schedule.[113]

A year after beginning the service, Woodson sublet the contract for the western end of the line from Fort Laramie to Salt Lake City to Feramorz Little. The plan was that the carriers should meet at the Fort on the fifteenth of the month and exchange consignments. For this service Little was to receive $8,000 per year. He hired Ephraim K. Hanks and Charles F. Decker to assist him. On the first trip Little and Hanks reached Fort Laramie in nine days, but with their mules so broken down they could not make the return journey. Obtaining five wild, unbroken ones they hitched them to the wagon. The first seven or eight miles were covered at runaway, breakneck speed. In September, 1851, Decker and Alfred Higgins were stopped at Box Elder Creek by a party of twenty Indians who plundered the wagon. During the four years of the contract, service between the Missouri River and Salt Lake City was fairly regular and satisfactory. Little and his associates met and conquered every difficulty an open road through seven hundred miles of virgin, unsettled territory could impose, Indian treachery and raids, inadequate pay, and they concluded their service with credit to themselves.[114]

William F. McGraw got the contract in 1854 for a four-year period. As before, the service was monthly but the remuneration was cut to $14,000. The mail was to be carried in four-horse coaches and the time was again thirty days. McGraw expected to carry on a passenger as well as a mail business. His rate was $180 to Salt Lake City and $300 to the Pacific Coast. This was not a success, however. Indians, who still infested the route, inflicted such damage upon the line that McGraw presented the House Committee on Post Offices and Post Roads with a claim for damages sustained on account of them. The Committee reviewed the case, approved the claim, and recommended that compensation for 1855

[113] Hafen, pp. 57-60.
[114] *Ibid.*

and 1856 be $36,000. It also stipulated that the contract should be annulled on August 18 of that year and that bids should be called for.[115]

The successful bidder in 1856 was Hiram Kimball of Salt Lake City, agent for Brigham Young and other Mormon leaders. The pay was $23,000 per year for a monthly service in carriages or wagons. The contract was let early in June, but prior to that and as early as February meetings were held in the Salt Lake City Tabernacle for the purpose of organizing a company to transport mail and freight. In one meeting Brigham Young offered to take stock in the concern and equip three hundred miles of the line himself. Others became interested and the Brigham Young Express Company was launched. One important item in the plan was to form settlements along the line where reserve animals could be kept, provisions could be collected, and weary travelers could rest if they wished to do so. To the Mormons these stations would have been of incalculable benefit, for the tide of immigration to Salt Lake Valley was running high at that time. Plans for all these things were pushed with vigor until the severe winter of 1856 compelled a halt in the work. It was begun again in 1857 but was terminated by the forwarding of United States troops to Utah.[116]

When service to Salt Lake City was resumed in 1857, S. B. Miles was given a contract to carry the mail from the Missouri River to Salt Lake City. The contract stipulated that the mail should be carried in coaches in the summer and on pack horses in the winter. The pay was $32,000 per year. Early in April, 1858, this contract was annulled and a new one made with Hockaday & Company for a weekly service in four-mule wagons or carriages on a twenty-two day schedule for $190,000.[117]

While Samuel H. Woodson and Feramorz Little were struggling to fulfill the conditions of their contract east of Salt Lake City, George Chorpenning and Absalom Woodward signed one in February, 1851, to carry the mail from that city to Sacramento, California. This put the United States mail in operation from end to end of the Central Route for the first time. The distance was about nine hundred miles, the pay $14,000 per year, and the time thirty days. On May 1 of that year Chorpenning left Sacramento with a party of men for the first trip. In the

---

[115] Root and Connelley, *Overland Stage to California*, p. 2; Hafen, *op. cit.*, pp. 60-61.
[116] Hafen, pp. 61-62.
[117] *Ibid.*

high Sierra they encountered snow so deep that they had to pound it down with wooden mauls so that the animals could travel. Through sixteen days and nights they toiled and camped under those conditions.

When the summer came they experienced difficulties with the Indians. In November Woodward was killed by a war party west of the Malad River in western Utah. In December the carriers were compelled to turn back on account of deep snow. The mail for February 1852, was routed through Feather River Pass and arrived at Salt Lake City in sixty days. The horses had frozen to death in the Goose Creek Mountains and the party had to travel the last two hundred miles on foot. In March the mail was sent by water to San Pedro, and thence through Cajon Pass and up the Mormon Trail to its destination. During the summer of 1852 it proceeded along the old trail via the Humboldt River, but when winter came on arrangements were made to forward it by way of Los Angeles. Chorpenning did his best to comply with the conditions of his contract but the Postmaster General did not fully understand the reasons for the various irregularities and delays. Therefore, he cancelled the contract and signed another with W. L. Blanchard of California late in 1852 for $50,000 per year. Upon learning of this Chorpenning went to Washington, got reinstated, his pay increased to $30,000, and permission to route the mail via San Pedro in the winter time.[118]

In 1854 Chorpenning was again the successful bidder. The route was changed to run from San Diego to Salt Lake City, the pay was $12,500 per annum, and the time twenty-eight days. Service was to begin on July 1 of that year and to continue for four years. During the summer, Indian difficulties arose again and the contractor began to lose money. In 1856 Congress acted in his behalf by increasing the pay to $30,000 per year until the contract expired in 1858. While it was in force the mails were carried on horseback with reasonable regularity and sometimes on less than schedule time. Chorpenning again received the contract in 1858. It provided for a semimonthly service of twenty days at $34,400 per year. Before July 1 it was ordered upon a weekly basis with sixteen days for the trip at $130,000. He bought ten stage coaches in the East, shipped them by water to Atchison, Kansas, where they were unloaded and driven across the Plains to Salt Lake City.[119]

118 *Ibid.*, pp. 63-70.
119 *Ibid.*

X

THE PONY TAKES OVER

AVING CREATED an organization capable of carrying all of the mail between the Missouri River and the West Coast over the Central Route, Russell's next concern was to forever silence the critics of that route by a practical demonstration of what could be done upon it. Apparently the method had been germinating in his mind for some time, in fact ever since early in 1858, according to his nephew, Charles R. Morehead Jr. This was a pony express. Alexander Majors said that Senator W. M. Gwin broached the idea to Russell in Washington in the winter of 1859 and that after various consultations he agreed to undertake it providing his partners would join him. Those consultations must have occurred *early* in 1859, for Russell was in the East after October and had no opportunity to consult his partners until February 1860.

There is no question but that the organization of the Pony Express was decided upon in October 1859, at the time the Leavenworth & Pike's Peak Express Company was taken over by Russell, Majors & Waddell, and that Russell returned to the East with the project in mind. That was one of the main reasons for taking over that bankrupt concern. On January 27, 1860, he telegraphed his son John W. at Leavenworth: "Have determined to establish a Pony Express to Sacramento, California, commencing 3d of April. Time ten days." John W. released the announcement to the newspapers, and the world had its first information concerning Russell's newest adventure.

The question of who originated the idea of the Pony Express, though debated ably and often, probably never will be conclusively settled. Morehead, in his honest, straightforward "Personal Recollections," says that Russell conceived the idea himself early in 1858 and discussed it with Secretary Floyd in the presence of himself and James Rupe. Glen D. Bradley's statement that "Mr. B. F. Ficklin, General Superintendent for the big freighting and stage firm of Russell, Majors & Waddell" spoke of it to Senator Gwin as the two were traveling along the Central Route in 1854 is wholly in error. The firm of Russell, Majors & Waddell did not exist in that year and did not engage in the stage business until 1859. Moreover, there is no record of Ficklin being connected with the firm until the latter year. The palm, therefore, evidently does not go to Ficklin.

Another and hitherto unrevealed story of its origin is told by John Scudder who relates that in the winter of 1859 he, A. B. Miller, and other employees of Russell, Majors & Waddell were at Salt Lake City. Upon reading the accounts of the overland mail controversy in newspapers reaching them, they became interested in the subject and began to figure time and distances on the Central Route. Being convinced that the mail could be carried on that route in much shorter time than upon the Southern, they wrote a letter to Russell informing him that they would undertake to carry it from St. Joseph to Sacramento in twelve days. Russell replied, asking for further information. In reply they drew a rough map of the proposed route and set down full particulars of their plan, which was to build stations and cover the route by relays of riders. They were so convinced of the practicability of their plan that A. B. Miller offered to test it on a trial run from the Missouri River to the Pacific Coast. The first notice they had of Russell's adoption of their idea was an order to Miller to buy two hundred head of good horses at Salt Lake City. Assisting Miller were B. F. Ficklin, Joseph A. Slade, James E. Bromley, and J. H. Clute. When the horses were purchased Scudder helped distribute them among the stations between Salt Lake City and Platte Bridge.[120]

This story bears the earmarks of an accurate, authentic account and dovetails perfectly with that of Morehead. The idea had lain dormant in Russell's mind for about a year. Letters from the group in Salt Lake City clinched it, so to speak, and galvanized him into action. The result was the Pony Express. Therefore both the original idea and the credit for putting it into operation probably belong to him more than to anyone else.

One other question remains: Why did he put the Pony Express into operation? The answer is not difficult to find. Certainly it was not because he thought the Pony Express would pay dividends. Both Majors and Waddell knew it would not. That was their sole objection to it.

---

[120] John Scudder, "The Pony Express," (Aug. 22, 1888). Majors, *Seventy Years on the Frontier*, p. 106.

Majors, three dozen years later, said that Senator Gwin asked him to start it "to test the practicability of crossing the Sierra Nevadas, as well as the Rocky Mountains, with a daily line of communications." That was close to the real reason but still somewhat off center from it. The practicability of crossing both mountain ranges in the winter time had already been conclusively demonstrated.

In a letter to Waddell some two months after the Pony Express was put into operation, Russell made some additional enlightening remarks.

I was disposed to make her (the Central Overland California & Pike's Peak Express Company) share a part of our heavy expense, and to do so most effectively I was compelled to build a world wide reputation, even at considerable expense (which all things considered is quite inconsiderate) and also to incur large expenses in many ways, the details of which I cannot commit to paper.[121]

That world-wide reputation being related to the express company and the effort to build it up being made early in 1860, he could have had reference to nothing save the Pony Express. With it as an advertising medium he hoped to so arouse and influence the public mind both in and outside Congress that opposition to the Central Route would be overthrown and a lucrative contract for carrying the United States mail would be given his Company.

Russell himself hastened to Missouri not long after he sent his telegram announcing the Pony Express, bringing the charter for the Central Overland California & Pike's Peak Express Company with him. It was presented to the Kansas Territorial Legislature early in February. There must have been some difficulty about it, perhaps because of its broad provisions, and considerable pressure had to be brought to bear to pass it. Waddell later scolded Russell for "buying the charter." [122] It was granted on February 20, 1860, and the company became a corporate body, the first of its kind with which Russell and his partners had had anything to do. Russell was elected president, Jerome B. Simpson vice-president, and John W. Russell secretary.

On March 20, 1860, Russell and Waddell, in behalf of the Central Overland California & Pike's Peak Express Company signed a contract with twenty representative citizens of St. Joseph, under which they agreed

---

[121] Russell to Waddell, June 19, 1860.
[122] Russell to Waddell, Aug. 15, 1860.

to establish an express office in St. Joseph and start coaches from there to Denver on a weekly schedule or oftener after May 1, 1860; to run a Pony Express from Wathena, Kansas, to Sacramento, California, as soon as the Roseport & Palmetto Railroad reached the former place; and to start a fast freight line from St. Joseph to Denver. It was also agreed that the company should not be required to operate the Pony Express longer than six months if it did not pay.[123]

In return the citizens of St. Joseph were to convey to the company a block of twelve lots in Patee Addition, eighteen lots in the town of Elwood, Kansas, and eighteen acres of land near the terminus of the Roseport & Palmetto Railroad. They also agreed to furnish a building at Fifth and Francis streets and a room for an office at Second and Francis, rent-free for one year. They further agreed that the Roseport & Palmetto Railroad should be in operation from St. Joseph to the town of Wathena by May 15, 1861, that free passage of express matter, officers, agents, and employees of the Company should be granted over it for twelve months, and that the exclusive privilege of carrying express over that road and its extensions should be granted for twenty years. It was further agreed that the railroad company would withhold all connections with any other road running west to Denver which did not grant the company the same privilege and that all ferriage across the Missouri River for express coaches, wagons, etc., should be free for two years.

Russell and his partners were now in a position to engage in a new enterprise—the railway express business. They knew as well as anyone else that the laying of steel rails across the plains and mountains would drive the great freight wagons and stage coaches from the road. Some day, they were convinced, a railroad would span the Central Route to the Pacific. When that time came they expected to operate an exclusive express business over it. If the infant Roseport & Palmetto Railroad fulfilled the expectations of its founders, that day was not far distant.

An office for the Central Overland California & Pike's Peak Express Company was opened in Washington at 481 Tenth Street, another in New York in the quarters of vice-president Jerome B. Simpson, No. 8, Continental Bank Building, Nassau Street, one in Chicago in charge of H. J. Spaulding as agent, and another in St. Louis in the office of Samuel & Allen. The home office and headquarters were at Leavenworth and in

[123] Contract between Citizens of St. Joseph, Mo., and Russell and Waddell, March 20, 1860.

charge of John W. Russell. Robert B. Bradford, who had represented the Leavenworth & Pike's Peak Express Company in Denver, gave way to J. B. Jones. In Salt Lake City an office was opened near the Mormon Tabernacle in charge of J. C. Bromley, and another in San Francisco in charge of William W. Finney.[124]

In the latter part of January Benjamin F. Ficklin went to Denver to close up the old Leavenworth & Pike's Peak Express Company and turn the business over to J. B. Jones. While there he arranged with Robert B. Bradford to build stage stations along the route as far west as Julesburg and to stock them with equipment and provisions. By March 15 he had them under construction and expected to have $20,000 to the credit of R. B. Bradford & Company when they were completed. He had also bought one hundred tons of hay, was having it baled, and was spending much money for the express company. Material for the construction of the stations and supplies for them were hauled in a Russell, Majors & Waddell wagon train under Wagonmaster Deering.[125]

Judging by R. B. Bradford & Company accounts against the express company no expense was spared in equipping the stations. Among the items sent out were brooms, candles, well wheels or pulleys, buckets, rope, window glass, doors, dishes, tinware for cooking, putty, horse brushes, curry combs, wagon grease, nails, screws, stovepipe, tin safes, scissors, axes, hammers, stovepipe dampers, etc. Food supplies included macaroni, dried fruits, flour, salt, pepper, pickles, tripe, syrup, sugar, coffee, tea, hams, bacon, beef, cloves, corn meal, raisins, mustard, etc. Common medicines for man and beast were copperas, alum, borax, turpentine, castor oil, etc.[126] Stations were being built and equipped from bases in Denver, Leavenworth, Salt Lake City, and Sacramento. When all were finished, there were 153 stations on the route. This did not include those from Julesburg to Denver.

When a station consisted of one room only it was generally divided by muslin curtains into kitchen, dining room, and living quarters. Upon a strong ridgepole reaching from side to side of the building, smaller poles were placed to make the foundation for a flat roof. Over these was laid a layer of willows, then straw, next dirt, and last of all a coat of

[124] Root and Connelley, *op. cit.*, pp. 107, 108. Bradford to Waddell, May 1, 1860.

[125] Bradford to Waddell, Jan. 26, Mar. 15, May 1, 3, 9, 14, 16, 1860.

[126] Central Overland California and Pike's Peak Express Company Dr. to R. B. Bradford & Co., 1860.

coarse gravel to keep the dirt from blowing away. This was the type of building constructed whether of logs, 'dobe, or sod. Some of them were half dugouts and others stood entirely above the ground. The buildings at Julesburg were the most elaborate along the whole route. The stations built by Bradford were of rough, green lumber sawed in the Rocky Mountains and covered with shingles. They, like those of the Leavenworth & Pike's Peak Express Company were of two kinds, "home" and "swing."

William W. Finney was just the man for getting the western end of the line into operation. He hired 21 men as express riders and packers, bought 129 mules, about 100 horses, and other necessary equipment such as saddles, bridles, blankets, tents, and provisions. Loading these into wagons, he struck out eastward along the route for Eagle Valley, establishing stations as he went. Those east of that place were to be set up and supplied from Salt Lake City by Major Howard Eagan. These stations were from twenty to twenty-five miles apart. Each rider was to travel from one to the other twice a week, traveling from thirty-five to seventy-five miles, using three horses. The average schedule was nine miles per hour day and night, allowing two minutes to change horses at each station. At Carson City, Bolivar Roberts also bought horses and hired men.[127]

The cost of getting the Central Overland California & Pike's Peak Express Company ready for operation must have been enormous. Frank A. Root said that it cost $75,000 to equip the Pony Express alone.[128] Since this project was only a part of the larger, more ambitious plan to operate stage coaches and a fast freight line, it is impossible to break the figures down into itemized schedules. Both stages, freight line, and Pony Express used the same facilities.

While stations were being built, horses for the Pony Express were being bought wherever animals which measured up to the high standard set by Russell could be found. On February 10, Jones, Russell & Company advertised in the Leavenworth *Daily Times* for "two hundred grey mares, from four to seven years old, not to exceed fifteen hands high, well broke to saddle, and warranted sound, with black hoofs, and suitable for run-

[127] Arthur Chapman, *The Pony Express*, pp. 33, 112, 113, 118, 131; Sage, *Out of the West*, p. 166.
[128] Chapman, p. 118.

ning the overland Pony Express." Some two hundred more were bought in Utah by A. B. Miller,[129] and others in California, Iowa, and Missouri. To fully equip the line, from four to five hundred were needed. These had to be young, sturdy, swift, and built for endurance. Getting the mail through on schedule time was not the only matter of prime importance. Carrying the rider to safety when pursued by Indians, which contingency was wisely foreseen, was of paramount concern. While serious difficulties with Indians were not expected, they were judiciously guarded against by the purchase of far better animals than the savages could boast. In the seventeen months the line operated more than one daring rider owed continued possession of his scalp to the excellent mount Russell had thoughtfully provided.

The saddles these tough horses bore upon their backs were especially designed for this service. Most of them were made by Israel Landis of St. Joseph, Missouri. They were lighter than the ordinary stock saddle used in the west, the cantle was low and sloping, the horn short and broad, and the skirt reduced to a minimum. Strength and lightness were prime considerations. Over the saddle, but completely detached from it, was thrown a broad, square, leather *mochila* with a hole for the horn and a slit for the cantle. At each corner was a *cantina* or box made of sole leather and equipped with a padlock for the mail. The combined weight of bridle, saddle, *mochila* and *cantinas* was thirteen pounds. Everything considered this was an ideal arrangement, for the *mochila,* when in place, became a part of the saddle and was held in place by the weight of the rider. This device also facilitated the changing of horses and riders at stations. All that was necessary at the end of a run was to strip the *mochila* from the incoming saddle and drop it over the outgoing one. Each rider used at least three different saddles upon a run but the *mochila* was passed from rider to rider like the stick in a relay race from St. Joseph to Sacramento and back.[130]

If Russell meant to startle and amaze the people of the country, both in the East and the West, by the announcements of the Pony Express, he admirably succeeded in his purpose. People had become accustomed to the idea of weeks and sometimes months being required for communication between California and the Atlantic Coast. To reduce that time

---

129 *Kansas Historical Quarterly,* XIV, 47.
130 Chapman, *op. cit.,* pp. 86-87.

to a few days seemed incredible. The announcement caused a "flutter" of concern among the friends and supporters of Butterfield and the Southern Route. Russell's friends greeted it with a roar of praise, knowing that if anyone could do it he could.

A little over two months after the announcement of the Pony Express startled the country, the line was ready to begin operations. A remarkable work of administration and organization had been done. Everything at St. Joseph was timed to the minute and a big send-off for the first rider was planned. A brass band was hired for the occasion and a great throng of people gathered in Patee Park across the street from the stable which housed the horses. Russell and Majors were there. Perhaps Waddell was also. The band played, and then speechmaking began. Mayor M. Jeff Thompson prophesied that the dust which enveloped the Pony Express rider would hardly die away before a puff of steam from a locomotive would be seen upon the horizon. Majors and Russell spoke briefly upon the benefits the undertaking would bestow upon the country, the prospects for the future, and its undoubted success. Majors also declared that the Pony Express was the predecessor of the railroad.[131]

The mail to be carried on this first westbound trip was made up in New York and forwarded to St. Joseph by rail on Saturday, March 31. By a stroke of misfortune a train connection was missed in Detroit. This would make it from two to four hours late in arriving at Hannibal, Missouri, 206 miles from St. Joseph.[132] Word of this was flashed to the latter place by telegraph. The band did its best to entertain the impatient crowd and everyone hoped the train on the new Hannibal & St. Joseph Railroad would make up the lost time.

Forty-nine letters wrapped in oiled silk to exclude moisture, five telegrams, and a few special editions of New York newspapers for Salt Lake City, Sacramento, and San Francisco made up the mail for this first trip. When the pouch containing it reached Hannibal it was placed upon the first railroad mail car ever built in the United States. The engineer of the wood-burner engine, named the *Missouri,* was Ad Clark. For the moment, the chief business of the entire line was to get that pouch to St. Joseph in the shortest possible time. Roadmaster George H. Davis ordered all trains off the main line, all switches locked, and fuel agents

131 *Ibid.,* p. 105.
132 *Ibid.,* p. 101.

at woodyards along the way to load the tender in record time. Engineer Clark was told to hang up a new speed record, one that would stand for fifty years. The pouch arrived at last and was put on board the train. Clark took his orders literally and pulled the throttle wide open. The *Missouri* responded nobly and leaped away upon her momentous cross-state run as though she understood the importance of this trip. When she came to a halt in St. Joseph to the accompaniment of cheers she had covered the distance in four hours and fifty-one minutes.[133] A remarkable record for that day.

Over at the stable the first pony, "a fine mare," was saddled, bridled, and ready to go. The rider, dressed in red shirt, blue pants, high top boots, and a wide brimmed plainsman's hat, was impatient to be off. Who this rider was has been the subject of debate for many years. The best direct evidence, an account in the *St. Joseph Weekly West* for April 7, 1860, states that he was "a Mr. Richardson, formerly a sailor, and a man accustomed to every degree of hardship." Frank A. Root, forty-one years later, said he was Johnny Frey and that the horse was jet black. So one takes his choice. At a quarter past seven, tall, lean Mayor Thompson swung the *mochila* into place, a cannon in the street before Patee House boomed, and the rider sped along the street to where the ferry boat Denver waited to set him across the Missouri River. On the Kansas side another cheering crowd awaited him. Passing through it he rode off into the night.[134] Ahead of him, all the way to the Pacific, men and animals tensely waited to carry that precious *mochila* to its destination.

While the people of St. Joseph put on a great celebration at the start of the first Pony Express rider those at San Francisco outdid them. This was natural since they were the ones who would profit most by rapid communication between the East and West and the establishment of a mail route over the Central Route. The line really ended at Sacramento, the head of navigation on the Sacramento River. Communication between that place and San Francisco was by boat. The promoters of the Pony Express and the people of San Francisco felt that a grand send-off for advertising and propaganda purposes was necessary. On the day of starting a great crowd turned out to see the "clean-limbed, hardy little nankeen-colored pony" leave the door of the Alta Telegraph Company's

133 Chapman, *The Pony Express*, pp. 102-104.
134 *Ibid.*, p. 103. Harlow, *Old Waybills*, p. 222.

office. While he waited somebody decorated him with miniature flags. Near by stood the first rider, ready to mount and dash off. Here again contemporaneous historians failed in their duty to posterity, for the records as to who he was are confusing. Some say he was James Randall and others that he was Harry Roff. Let it be as may, the affair in San Francisco was merely the first act of the show; the second would be staged when the first mail arrived from St. Joseph. The *mochila* bearing eighty-five letters was put in place, the rider mounted the pony from the wrong side, and galloped off. His journey, whoever he was, soon ended at the river where the mail was placed on board a steamer. Between two and three o'clock in the morning of April 4, the steamer docked at Sacramento and the mail was turned over to William Hamilton, the next rider. With no celebration and nobody to see him off, except fellow employees of the company, he rode off into the dark, rainy night, with Placerville, forty-five miles away, as his destination.[135] He reached it on schedule time and the Pony Express was off to a good start at both ends.

When the sturdy riders left St. Joseph and Carson City, the eastern and western ends of the Pacific telegraph lines, the heavy, impenetrable silence of the broad plains and mountains enveloped the enterprise. The westbound rider reached Salt Lake City at 11:45 P.M. on April 7, and the eastbound one at 6:25 on the 9th.[136] They met somewhere on the road west of that city on the 8th. Since no record of that historic meeting has been unearthed, one can only speculate upon what those two young men said to each other in the moment or two of greeting they must have indulged themselves. At that point the bridging of almost two thousand miles of plains, deserts, and mountains was actually completed. From there on, each covered the road already traveled by his predecessor going in the opposite direction.

It would be interesting to follow the riders through the months to come, the story of the Pah-Ute war in the early summer of 1861, and to describe their adventures. These and many other things, however, have been faithfully recorded by others. The completion of the first rides electrified the nation and was noticed in foreign newspapers. Down in Washington cloakrooms buzzed with talk of it, and friends of a mail line over the Central Route took heart. A few weeks after the Pony Express was

[135] Chapman, pp. 113-119.
[136] *Ibid.*, p. 132.

put into operation, a special Committee reported in favor of a railroad over the Route along the Platte Valley to Salt Lake City. On May 11 the Postmaster General annulled Chorpenning's mail contract over the western end of the Route, alleging failure to fulfill it, and awarded a semi-monthly service to the Central Overland California & Pike's Peak Express Company. This was a triumph of considerable proportions, for that company now held a monopoly upon mail service over the entire length of the Central Route and was in a favorable position to compete with the Overland Mail Company. Without a doubt this was in part the first fruits of the Pony Express.

Russell's magnificent dream of spanning the vast, forbidding distance between the Missouri River and the Pacific Coast in ten days came true in glorious fashion. The outburst of praise which greeted the accomplished fact was far greater than that following the inauguration of stage coach service between Leavenworth and Denver about a year before. During the months of its service, including about 150 round trips, it ran upon such a smooth schedule that critics of the Central Route were forever silenced. Before the winter of 1860-61 was past, even the most stubborn irreconcilables had to admit that stage coaches could run where the swift ponies galloped.

During those tragic days immediately preceding the outbreak of the Civil War the Pony Express constituted an important link between the East and West. To say that it alone saved California to the Union is being too liberal with praise, but there can be no doubt about its function in keeping the people informed concerning the march of events and in mobilizing patriotic sentiment in the Far West. Important government dispatches, messages from Washington to Territorial officials, private letters, and newspapers with the record of daily happenings, all sped across the continent in those little *cantinas*.

The Pony Express was a romantic, glorious, yet brief incident, which, although it proved nothing except that it could be done, is eminently worthy of remembrance. Even though the amount of mail it carried was relatively insignificant and out of proportion to the fame it achieved, nobody begrudges it the spotlight. The tattoo of the flying hoofbeats, awakening the echoes by day and night along the two-thousand-mile stretch of boundless prairie, lonely canyon, and mountain slope, wrote into the body of strictly American folklore such a romantic tale of youth-

Advertisement from the *Leavenworth City Directory*, 1859-60

Advertisement from the *Directory of Kansas City*, 1860, p. 54

ful grit as is given few peoples to possess. It has been the source of a thousand tales of daredevil courage and will continue to make its contribution to that thrilling body of literature which concerns itself with stark courage and dauntless enterprise. Brief though it was, it added the names of William H. Russell, Alexander Majors, William Bradford Waddell, William F. (Buffalo Bill) Cody, Pony Bob Haslam, Boston Kelly, and others to the honor roll of American heroes. That was the most important thing Russell and his partners got for their money. Unfortunately for them, it remained for later generations to understand and appreciate what was bought with their efforts and sacrifice.

It has been said again and again that the Pony Express ruined Russell, Majors & Waddell. That is not true. It was a failure as a financial asset from the beginning and made its contribution to the final debacle, but that contribution was both minor and one of many. The Central Overland California & Pike's Peak Express Company which operated it was also a failure as a money-making institution. So were most of the other partnerships with which those men were concerned, such as Miller, Russell & Company, R. B. Bradford & Company, Smoot, Russell & Company. The freighting business appears to be the only one which paid dividends. Had they confined their efforts to that and been reimbursed for their losses in 1857, the story probably would have been different. The stores operated by the firm in Lexington and Leavenworth probably made money, but it was not sufficient to change the inexorable march of events. The day Russell decided to organize the Leavenworth & Pike's Peak Express Company was a day of doom. That organization and its greater successor did as much to bankrupt the partners as the failure of the government to reimburse them for their losses in 1857.

XI

RUSSELL VS. FICKLIN

NOT LONG after the Pony Express was put into operation, Russell returned to his grinding duties in the East. He probably would have preferred remaining in the West where cheering crowds of admirers surrounded him, but he had work to do. The burden of financing the Central Overland California & Pike's Peak Express Company fell largely upon the firm of Russell, Majors & Waddell and a constant flow of large sums of money had to be maintained. In addition he had to have a mail contract over the Central Route. Others could run the Pony Express, the fast freight line to Denver, and the Concord coaches, but nobody could substitute for him in Washington. Although his name was rapidly becoming a household word all over the nation and congratulations were being showered upon him from President Buchanan down to the lowliest private citizen, his heart was heavy with foreboding in the early summer of 1860. It is one of those grim strokes of fortune that the man who had more to do with that famous institution than anyone else had the least time or reason for deriving satisfaction from the universal praise its success aroused. Regardless of the fact that no expense had been spared to insure the success of the Express Company, he knew that the practice of economy was imperative. Consequently when Benjamin F. Ficklin appeared in Washington about the middle of May and proposed a semi-weekly Pony Express he flatly vetoed it.[137]

This apparently ignited a smoldering difficulty between Ficklin and Russell. Perhaps the real matter at issue was the inevitable clash between two aggressive, efficient personalities. Whatever it may have been, it was serious and irreconcilable from the beginning. Ficklin went back west to his duties as route superintendent but the quarrel continued. Early in June, on account of two letters Russell wrote John S. Roberson of the St. Joseph office, Ficklin telegraphed his resignation. "Send a man for my

[137] Russell to Waddell, May 11, 1860.

place damned quick," he added.[138] This infuriated Russell and shocked his religious principles. On the 6th he wired to Waddell, Majors, and John S. Jones, quoted Ficklin's telegram, and instructed them to make J. H. Clute route superintendent. Since nothing was done about it, he telegraphed Waddell again on the 12th urging him to call a meeting of the board of directors to accept Ficklin's resignation and appoint Clute.[139]

This time Waddell was in no mood to obey Russell's instructions. He had a very high regard for Ficklin and was probably tired of being pushed about by his partner. Upon receipt of this message he wrote Russell a letter saying that Central Overland California & Pike's Peak Express Company could not get along without Ficklin. This further angered Russell and he wrote,

So far as I am concerned, if he were the only living man in the world (which I do not believe) that would put it through, and without him the Co. must sink and all be lost, I would say let him go by all means. . . . . If his resignation is not accepted and some other good man put in his place, my resignation is before you and my stock for sale.

On the same day he wrote Waddell another letter saying that he understood Ficklin would be in Washington on the following Friday to bid for a mail contract for the company. "From that," he said, "I infer that you retain him. If so, all right. I cannot cooperate with him." [140]

On June 9, probably after being reprimanded by Waddell, Ficklin wrote Russell a letter of apology. This might have healed the breach between them and restored harmony in the company had not Waddell written Russell a letter on the 11th which was like salt in a wound.

Your letter of the eleventh from St. Joe [Russell raged] is of such a character that I cannot longer consent to represent the Express Company in any shape. If after all my toil and sacrifice I am to be really *abused* for my course, it is high time that some other and more competent man be placed at the head of it. . . . . Hope the appointment of an agent to represent the Co. will be telegraphed today or tomorrow. Smoot is here and would doubtless be glad to act. Ficklin in whom you all have so much confidence is expected today. . . . Would rather dig for my bread than work and live as I have for the past six months. . . . I am confident of one thing, however, and that is with all Mr. Ficklin's boasted economy, if allowed to control as you say he must,

138 Russell telegram to Waddell, Jones, and Majors, June 6, 1860.
139 Russell telegram to Waddell and Executive Committee, July 12, 1860.
140 Russell to Waddell, June 13, 1860 (2 letters).

the Co. will break up in 12 months. My stock is for sale, first to the Co. as agreed upon, next to you and Mr. M., and if neither want it then to any outsider who will pay you cash or secure you to your satisfaction . . . at a valuation of $500,000.00.

This letter so alarmed Waddell and John S. Jones that they hurried a conciliatory telegram off to Russell. He read it on the 19th, felt a load lifted from his heart and sat down to pour out his harassed soul in a long letter. It reveals so much of the man and his affairs that it may be quoted here.

Your letter and that of John S. Jones, together with Ficklin's and Smoot's, various reports, received at a time when I was crushed to earth. The load prior to their receipt was all that I could bear. . . . A failure to meet our paper, and especially that accepted by the War Department, I knew would end in our everlasting disgrace, one from which we could (nor can we) never rise even after (as we could and should) we have paid up the last dollar for which we might be liable. . . . Knowing that you and Mr. Majors felt the great importance of sustaining at least an untarnished reputation, and knowing too that the Express Co. had in a measure brought about the state of things, I was disposed to make her share a part of our heavy burdens. . . . When your letter came complaining of extravagance and actually intimating that my course would not be approved either by R. M. and W. or the Express Co., I was verily crushed. . . . My dear sir, if you will but calmly reflect for an hour on my true position, you would almost cry for me (if that would do any good.) I pass a most miserable life, exiled from my family. . . . My dear sir, money could not induce me to do this. 'Tis our reputation, our honor, the latter I hold dearer than life, that now sustains and prompts me to thus seemingly abandon home and family and all social enjoyment for a miserable life here in Washington. . . . I am now stimulated by the sole desire of saving our sinking fortunes and more especially our honor. . . . Give me poverty with an untarnished reputation in place of fortune obtained through dishonorable course. I am aware that if we are forced to suspend we have committed no crime legally or morally, yet the censorious world would attach moral guilt, and all we could do would not relieve us. . . . The dispatch from Waddell and Jones of today is a source of much satisfaction. I accept it as wiping out the past.

The difficulty between the partners was harmoniously adjusted but Russell did not change his attitude toward Ficklin. In the same letter he said,

I cannot, will not consent to his again taking charge as Superintendent. He is too self-willed. Will rule or ruin. . . . As for economy he knows it not, and not only so, he has nothing to lose in the way of money. His only desire seems to be to get up a big name (at our expense) for a splendid line and expeditiously run. . . . Why? Simply because he is down on one of our stockholders, (one too who had done more to save all than all the rest put together) he would circumvent me if possible, blow the whole thing to gratify his unlawful ambition to rule or ruin.

The quarrel with Ficklin was an unfortunate affair. Everyone else associated with him, including unbiased Robert B. Bradford, considered him a valuable man. Waddell suggested that they adjust matters and make up, to which Russell indignantly replied,

Socially I cannot, will not in a business sense. My resolution is as fixed as the law of Medes and Persians. . . . I have read your letter to Simpson and do think you done me a great injustice saying I was just like Ficklin, must ride the lead horse or not go at all. . . . One thing is sure and that is unless things can be moved more agreeable between partners I cannot and will not act longer. Would rather see it all sunk with my future prospects than go through such a hell another month.

In the end he had his way and Ficklin's resignation was accepted about the first of July.

The best index to the financial status of Russell and his partners in the summer of 1860 is his remarks in his letters to Waddell, May 11.

As our securities are being cut down and nothing with which to base a negotiation east and as such have been casting around to see what we could do, and I see nothing left except our Express stock. Send mine to me at once in New York and I will try to see if it can be used as collateral. Think that $50,000.00 might be borrowed on it for 12 mo. and if it can be done had better use yours and Mr. M[ajors'] also.

[May 12]   Must have help. . . . Have $150,000.00 to pay next week and quite a large portion the middle of the week. Have about $60,000.00 on hand. S[amuel] and A[llen] will likely send $40,000.00 more . . . really fighting so many hopes and fears I cannot be efficient at W[ashington].

[June 19]   If all things work right and you will aid me from the west I will see this firm out of trouble, over the shoals and quicksands and move our vessel in a safe harbor. . . .

[June 22]   New York June payments provided for, but how to arrange for July I know not. Cannot certainly unless you and Samuel and A[llen] come up liberally. If all things work along smoothly . . . . our good credit east and west will sustain us, if on the other hand we get to jarring and break up our companies or cripple them [it] will effect us materially even if it does not result in a break up.

[June 29] Now is the pinch of the game and I fear results. If we can get along 30 days the rubicon is passed and we are all safe. When I wrote you so confidently from New York on the 19th I then fully expected to draw the P. O. money $127,000.00 which failed. Also relied confidently on Cherique. That too was lost. Our accounts are largely over[due] in New York and large amounts to pay tomorrow and all next week, which cannot be done without aid from L[eavenworth] and St. Louis. . . . Will make any sacrifice before going down, but really fear it cannot be raised. Will do my utmost. It would be awful to go down now after so much sacrifice and vexation, and too when we have such good prospects ahead with which to pay out.

[June 30] Harried to death now about money. Know not where to turn or how it will result. . . . No reply from Mr. Waddell. Cannot exist without aid.

[July 8] I am waiting on one claim hope to put through and off Wednesday 11th. Will the first moment that is settled. Without it cannot go through July. With it think I can with your aid and promises. Simpson is having an awful time just now keeping things alive. . . . How unfortunate that 6/10 or more of our entire debt falls due in this next month.

[July 10] How Simpson gets along I cannot tell. I do know that half our paper, including Sec'y acceptances maturing in the last ten days has had to lay over till next day, such was the case yesterday. . . . You must hurry remittances. Must aid as we must not go under.

[August 5] You must not neglect those renewals and obtain all that is possible on new loans in addition. You cannot negotiate and remit too much. We will want large aid in Sept. and as the approach of fall the money market will tighten up. You must aid liberally. I cannot carry the load alone, and indeed I will not try.

[August 13] You must hurry up remittance and those renewals. We cannot get along without it. Do not allow a single day to pass, urge discounts in every quarter.

Russell's "good prospects ahead with which to pay out" lay in a new mail contract over the Central Route. Although Congress had adjourned without doing anything in that direction he hoped to get it anyway. Senator Gwin, who had always worked for the overland mail, pursued what seemed to many a peculiar course in that session. He supported none of the various measures offered, some of which showed signs of passing, and stuck to his own to the last. The *San Francisco Bulletin* accused him of being persuaded by the Administration to contribute to the defeat of the most promising of these by assurances that after Congress adjourned a semi-weekly mail between St. Joseph and Placerville on a twenty-day schedule would be authorized by the Post Office Department. On June 13 Russell wrote Waddell:

I am in treaty for tri-weekly mail at $600,000.00 which have hope of closing today. And although it will pay very handsome it is not as good as we wanted. It will however lay the foundation for a mail which will give us $1,200.000.00.

On the 22d he said:

Do not think any mail service will pass Congress and as the appropriation for the P. O. Dep't. has cut off the ocean service of course the Dep't will be freed to contract with us and at a good price. Will lay still until Congress adjourns, which will be tomorrow or Monday, then get to work for the contract. The service must be had. Butterfield wrote cannot and dare not undertake it. They now rest on a contract made by Congress which the latter are disposed to break up and as such Butterfield and Co. are not disposed to tamper with it before the Dep't. We will certainly get a good thing.

On July 8 he still felt confident he would secure the contract.

If we get the service ordered up our pay to Salt Lake is $250,000.00. Time through 25 days. I shall let the old contractor take the west end from Salt Lake. 'Tis a nuisance to us.

The contract Russell offered to make with the Post Office Department for carrying the mail from St. Joseph to Folsom, California, three times a week on a twenty-five day schedule, called for $900,000 pay the first year. After that it would be six times a week for the same amount. Early in June, Senator Gwin sought to press the matter to a conclusion by addressing a letter to the President.

I was induced to believe, from conversations with you and the Postmaster General that if public necessity required you would have the mails—letters as well as printed matter—carried overland if Congress failed to legislate further on the subject. The necessity has arisen.

On June 10 Russell wrote Waddell and mentioned the Pony Express for the first time since May 11.

> With regard to the Pony. The result is to be regretted. I am only delaying action 'til mail facilities are decided. True, I have not much hope, but may carry it. At all events today's cabinet settles the question.

The cabinet meeting of July 10, 1860, did indeed settle the question. Russell's bid for a contract was brushed aside and nothing whatever done in regard to a mail line over the Central Route. That meeting marked the beginning of the end for Russell, Majors & Waddell. On that day the dissolution of their vast transportation empire was assured. Now nothing, even the most desperate of measures, which were taken, could save the firm.

In midsummer, 1860, there was no arrangement whatever for carrying the United States mail to the Rocky Mountain region except as express matter in the Central Overland California & Pike's Peak Express Company's coaches. By July 1 this was averaging five thousand letters per week. In that month Hinckley Express Company, which ran a line of stages from Denver into the mountains, paid the former company almost $6,000.00 in fees for letters and newspapers it carried.[141]

About this time the Post Office Department gave attention to a regular mail line to that region. E. F. Bruce of St. Joseph was given a contract for carrying it from that place to Julesburg, where it was then to be taken by the Central Overland California & Pike's Peak Express Company's coaches to Denver. For some reason this arrangement was not carried out, and on August 29 a new one was made with E. S. Alford of the Western Stage Company for a weekly mail from Fort Kearny to Denver.[142] It is probable that the quarrel between Russell and Ficklin, with whom the first arrangement was made in Washington, accounted for Bruce's failure.

Having a stage line already in operation from Fort Kearny to Omaha, the Western Stage Company now became a dangerous competitor of the Central Overland California & Pike's Peak Express Company. To make matters worse, when the former's coaches began running into Denver

---

[141] Hafen, *Overland Mail*, p. 159. *Lawrence Republican*, July 26, 1860. *New York Tribune*, Aug. 25, 1860.

[142] Guckert telegram to John W. Russell, July 16, 1860. W. H. Russell to Waddell, Aug. 25, 1860.

about the middle of August, 1860, the Hinckley Express Company established a special express messenger service over its line to Omaha.[143] This broke the express monopoly Russell and his associates had enjoyed since the opening of the Leavenworth & Pike's Peak Express Company more than a year before. When the first United States mail arrived in Denver about the middle of August under the Bruce agreement, it was carried in Russell's coaches. On August 14 the first eastbound mail under ordinary postage rates went out in the same manner. These two consignments alone deprived the Central Overland California & Pike's Peak Express Company of about $3,500 in fees. It was said at the time that this Company was paid the nominal sum of $800 for carrying the mail from Julesburg to Denver under the Bruce contract, which was about one twentieth of what it cost. Although this was done to shut out competition in the express business, the fact remained that a rival line operated from Denver to Omaha. Under the express messenger plan inaugurated by the Hinckley Express Company the Western Stage Company was by early fall carrying from $80,000 to $100,000 worth of gold to Omaha per month.[144]

The state of affairs confronting Russell in relation to the passenger, express, and mail business to the Rocky Mountain country in midsummer of 1860 was serious indeed. In the latter part of July he went to Leavenworth for a meeting of the board of directors of the Central Overland California & Pike's Peak Express Company. The answer to the problems confronting them was a drastic reduction in rates and an increase of speed along the line. Passenger fares from St. Joseph to Denver were cut from $100 to $75, the fee for letters from twenty-five cents to ten, and the time reduced from twelve to six days. In December additional reductions were announced.[145]

These things, embarrassing though they were, did not affect the service rendered by the Central Overland California & Pike's Peak Express Company. While it was almost an insupportable liability to the freighting firm, its service was praised by its clients. Said the *Rocky Mountain News:*

This old pioneer line still continues the even tenor of its way, winning popularity and steadily growing in public favor . . . it stands today, probably

[143] Hafen, p. 160.

[144] *Lawrence Republican,* July 26, 1860. *Kansas Historical Quarterly,* XIV, 73. *New York Tribune,* Sept. 28, 1860.

[145] *New York Tribune,* Sept, 28, 1860.

the best fitted, best stocked and best managed route of the same magnitude in the world. . . . Unlike the Butterfield route, with its subsidy from the government of $600,000 per year for carrying the mails, this colossal enterprise has been built up and is wholly sustained by private enterprise. The benefits that have accrued to this country from its establishment would be hard to estimate and can hardly be overrated. It is doubtful whether we would at any time prior to July last have been favored with any kind of mail facilities had it not established and maintained its line for many months, with actual heavy loss. Its projector and president, William H. Russell, well deserved the name of "Napoleon of the West." [146]

[146] Hafen, *Overland Mail,* pp. 161-162.

XII

THE BOND SCANDAL

W HEN the contract for freighting on the New Mexico Route for 1860-61 was signed, everyone thought that trains carrying supplies to military posts in the Southwest would be started at the usual time, in May and June. This, however, was not done. Week after week, Russell, Majors & Waddell waited for notices of transportation required, but they did not come. The effect of this delay by the War Department was nothing short of catastrophic. It compelled the firm to pay wages to idle men and care for thousands of oxen, impaired the firm's credit, and made it impossible to meet loans falling due in midsummer which had been negotiated upon the promise of being repaid with funds earned in transportation.[147] The bulk of supplies was ordered out in August and September, which meant that most of the pay would be received the latter part of September, at the earliest, fully six months after obligations based upon the usual practice fell due. Three factors, therefore, expense of organizing and operating the Central Overland California & Pike's Peak Express Company and the Pony Express, failure to secure the great mail contract, and delay in forwarding military supplies to the Southwest, combined to create an utterly hopeless situation.

While this crisis was at its height Russell went to New York early in July with the hope that relief might be obtained there. In addition to obligations already past due, there was some $200,000 worth of acceptances maturing the latter part of the month, and he had no money with which to meet them.[148] This trip to New York was not helpful, mainly because James T. Soutter, his financial mainstay in that city, had been confined to his home by sickness since March. The situation, though deadly in its portents, was simple. Russell, Majors & Waddell owed everybody who had credited them in the past so much that he could not expect further accommodations, and sinister whispers concerning the firm's

---

[147] Russell to Samuel & Allen, Sept. 29, 1860.
[148] *H.R.*, 36th Cong., 2d sess., Report 78, p. 334.

solvency were already worming their poisonous way through financial circles.

After a fruitless day or two in New York, Russell took the train back to Washington on July 11. On it he found his friend, Luke Lea, member of the Washington banking firm of Suter, Lea & Company. Lea had been Commissioner of Indian affairs from 1850 to 1853. Luther R. Smoot, Russell's partner in Smoot, Russell & Company, was also a member of this firm. Being more or less familiar with each other's business affairs, they fell to talking about the crisis confronting Russell, Majors & Waddell. Russell frankly confessed his critical situation and inquired of Lea whether he could aid him in securing enough money to meet the acceptances about to fall due. When Lea replied in the negative, Russell then asked him if he knew of anyone in Washington who could lend him money or securities. Lea's reply was that he did not believe that amount could be raised in the capital. Russell then remarked that while in New York he had heard of a man by the name of "Baylor" who might be a prospect. Lea said he did not know of a man by that name but did know one named Godard Bailey who had dealt in Florida bonds. Although "as poor as anybody" he was a man of high legal attainments. Since his wife was the daughter of a cousin of Secretary of War John B. Floyd, he might be useful in getting claims paid by that Department. Russell then requested Lea to see Bailey as soon as possible and inform him as to the situation and the danger to the Secretary should the acceptances be protested.[149]

Upon arriving in Washington, Lea went to his bank and Russell to the War Department to see whether he could collect $75,000 to $100,000 which he said was due his firm. Late that afternoon, July 12, he also went to the bank and asked Lea whether he had seen Bailey. Lea said he had not, but would probably see him the next day, which he did. Bailey probably went to the War Department immediately after this interview, where he talked with William R. Drinkard, chief clerk. He understood, he said, that Russell was in a "tight place" and that there was a probability that some of Secretary Floyd's acceptances would be protested. If that were true, he wished to know what effect it would have upon Floyd. When Drinkard replied that it would disturb him greatly, Bailey remarked that if he could be entirely satisfied concerning Russell's respon-

---

[149] H.R., 36th Cong., 2d sess., Report 78, pp. 45, 46, 50, 52, 53, 100, 334.

sibility he thought he could accomplish a negotiation which would relieve him.[150]

Drinkard's reply was that he had better see Russell, who was in the building at the time. A few minutes later he introduced them and left them to themselves. Bailey seems to have come to the point immediately by asking Russell whether the facts he had learned from Drinkard were correct and whether the acceptances being protested would result in disgrace for Secretary Floyd. When Russell replied in the affirmative, Bailey asked what amount was required to clear the situation. The reply was that $150,000 would do it nicely. Upon hearing this, Bailey said that his mind was made up. He had some state securities which were at Russell's disposal on condition that they be only hypothecated and the identical bonds returned. Russell assured him this would certainly be done. Consequently at two o'clock that afternoon Bailey delivered $150,000 worth of Missouri and Tennessee state bonds to Russell at his home in Potentini's rooming house and took his note on Russell, Majors & Waddell for that amount.[151]

That afternoon Russell took the train for New York, carrying the bonds with him. Next day in company with Jerome B. Simpson he borrowed $50,000 from what he called the "Chatham Bank," leaving Russell, Majors & Waddell's notes, one for seventy and the other ninety days, and the bonds as security.[152] The remainder was left with Simpson to dispose of immediately upon the best terms he could. Securing the bonds from Bailey so eased his financial situation that he could make a hurried trip back West to attend the meeting of the board of directors of the Central Overland California & Pike's Peak Express Company in Leavenworth the latter part of the month.

Undoubtedly Russell told Majors and Waddell, if the former were not out upon the Plains as usual, about the new and unexpected source of money he had more or less accidentally discovered. There was no reason why he should have kept it secret. What he said encouraged them to hope they would be able to ride out the storm.

By August 13 he was back in New York. On that day a railroad train of thirty-five cars loaded exclusively with goods and groceries he had bought for the firm left that place and steamed toward the West. While

[150] *Ibid.*, pp. 54, 55, 119, 120.
[151] *Ibid.*, pp. 29, 150, 264, 325.
[152] *Ibid.*, pp. 235, 265, 266.

he was away his financial condition deteriorated day by day. Jerome B. Simpson had done his best with the state bonds, but since they were worth only about fifty to sixty cents upon the dollar the whole lot brought in only about $97,000, a sum wholly inadequate to resolve the crisis.[153]

Back in Washington in September, Russell again attempted to collect money from the War Department, but failed. Not knowing what else to do he sent Godard Bailey a note asking him to come and see him the following evening. When Bailey arrived he found the place filled with Russell's friends, who had probably assembled to welcome him back to Washington. Taking him aside, Russell bluntly informed him that Russell, Majors & Waddell was still financially embarrassed, that some of the previous bonds were about to be sold on the open market, that $300,000 more of Secretary Floyd's acceptances were about to mature, and that owing to the financial condition of the country, especially in the West, he could not raise sufficient money to redeem the bonds. Then of the shocked Bailey he inquired whether he knew of any way in which he could lend further assistance.[154]

This confession of financial impotence on the part of Russell must have staggered the obscure clerk in the Department of the Interior. But he was not the only one to receive shattering information. In reply he confessed that the bonds he had given Russell belonged to the Indian Trust Fund of the Department of the Interior of which he was merely the custodian. These bonds represented unpaid annuities to various Indian tribes and were not the property of the government even. In plain, everyday terms, Bailey was an embezzler in the amount of $150,000. In his statement to the Select Committee of the House, dated January 16, 1861, Russell said he had "no knowledge whatever that he [Bailey] was a government officer, or that the bonds belonged to the government. I supposed he had a perfect right to control them, and no questions were asked by me and nothing said by him in regard to the ownership of them."[155]

There is no reason whatever for disbelieving this statement. When the transaction was consummated, Russell naturally assumed that Bailey had the right to hold or surrender the bonds at his own discretion. More-

153 *H.R.,* 36th Cong., 2d sess., Report 78, p. 268.
154 *Ibid.,* p. 271.
155 Russell, "Public Statement," Mar. 28, 1861.

over, there is absolutely nothing in Russell's previous history to warrant doubt as to his veracity in this instance. Speculator, even to the point of recklessness at times, he indeed was, but a dishonest man never. Luther R. Smoot, who knew him intimately as a business man, characterized him accurately when he said, "Mr. R[ussell], full of honesty himself—he presumes others as full as himself and thus the wolves would filch from him thousands and give no equivalent therefor." [156] It is idle to speculate upon why Bailey did not frankly tell him the truth about the bonds in the beginning. Perhaps he knew Russell's reputation for integrity and, moved by a reckless desire to protect Secretary Floyd, dared not reveal their true ownership lest Russell spurn them, which he certainly would have done. In the initial transaction between them, not so much as a shadow can justly be cast upon his motives.

Bailey told Russell that unless the bonds were returned he was a ruined man. In his statement for the newspapers, published April 4, 1861, Russell said,

This disclosure [of the ownership of the bonds[completely overwhelmed me. It added entanglement to my embarrassment. I saw instantly and with intense reality, how difficult it would be to extricate myself from my unfortunate dilemma. . . . When I discovered that the bonds belonged to the Indian Trust Fund I would have freely given the whole of this large claim (for losses in Utah in 1857), and everything I was worth besides, to have been able at that moment to restore them. Other acceptances of the War Department were then maturing and would likely go to protest. This I knew would so impair the credit of our firm as to render the sale of the bonds certain and their recovery impossible. I had no time to devote to calm reflection. A week or ten days might have enabled me to mature some plan by which to recover and restore them, but, in the meantime they were likely to be sold. . . . In the stress of my difficulties, I was in no condition, and, as I have said before, I had no time to weigh the responsibility, on the one hand of wrecking our firm, discrediting the War Department, and permitting the hypothecated bonds to be sold beyond my reach, against that on the other hand of accepting more bonds with which to protect those that I had already used. . . . I determined upon the latter alternative.[157]

One who has followed Russell's unique, colorful, and sometimes brilliant business career from the beginning regrets to face the remainder

[156] Smoot to Waddell, Dec. 18, 1860.
[157] *St. Louis Tri-Weekly Republican*, Apr. 4, 1861.

of the story concerning the bond transactions. Next day Bailey, after cutting off the January 1860 coupons, delivered $387,000 worth of Missouri, South Carolina, and Florida Trust Fund bonds to Russell. He also returned the Russell, Majors & Waddell note for $150,000 and took another for the full amount, $537,000. The only condition was that the bonds be hypothecated and the full number returned before March 4, 1861, when Bailey's term of office expired.[158] By this act Russell fully shared Bailey's guilt. Whether he was morally guilty in the first instance might be debatable, but certainly not in the second. By his own frank, straightforward confession he convicts himself of receiving and using for his own purposes property he knew was stolen.

That night Russell hurried off for New York where he undertook to hypothecate the new lot of bonds. The Missouri and North Carolina issues were readily accepted, at a discount, but nobody would so much as look at those of Florida. Lee, Higginson & Company of Boston loaned $40,000 on $60,000 worth of South Carolinas, and others were negotiated through William F. Coleman of the United States Trust Company of New York, E. S. Darling & Company, Duncan, Sherman & Company, and others. What he got for the two hundred Missouris is not known. The long, tragic shadow of the Civil War was already creeping across the nation and the securities market was plunging downward. Since he could not dispose of the Floridas, he took them back to Bailey and received a like number of North Carolinas.[159]

When he secured the second lot of bonds from Bailey, he assured him that they would enable him to recover the first ones, sustain the credit of Russell, Majors & Waddell, and redeem Secretary Floyd's acceptances. But again the amount he realized upon them fell far short of the requirement. By the latter part of September he was finished. His swan song was a letter to Samuel & Allen of St. Louis on September 29.

> I have failed in my negotiations to the amount required. . . . To carry the immense business and interests of R. M. and W. to a successful realization and termination enabling them to take up some $70,000.00 now under protest, and meet all future engagements as they mature will require a loan or renewal of four hundred thousand dollars to be extended say one third cash maturing in May, June, and July. With this sum they can be sustained, and not only

158 *H.R.*, 36th Cong., 2d sess., Report 78, pp. 194, 240, 272, 336.
159 *Ibid.*, pp. 273, 274, 275, 276.

Conestoga Wagon
(*Courtesy of the Museum of Science and Industry, Chicago*)

Train Books

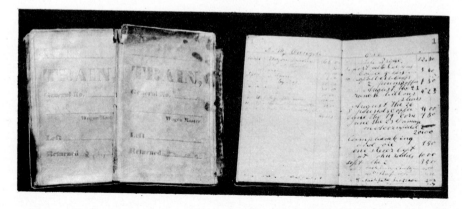

so but can be the means of sustaining a vast number of debtors to Bank(s) and Bankers in St. Louis and upper Mo. . . . Again if we are sustained it will enable the Express Co., of which we are large stockholders, to secure the mail pay of $129,000.00 now due them under actual and bona fide contract now withheld by the P.M. General awaiting the action of Congress, of which we are assured by numbers of prominent members of all political parties shall be done next winter. . . . If we suspend the influence we have so long enjoyed will be lost and with it I fear that amount justly due our Express Company. . . . And also the influence of our large claim (of over $400,000.00) now before Congress. At present our prospects for getting it next winter (if a president is elected by the people) is good, but as you know would be the case, let us suspend and be reported as a failing or doubtful concern, and the claim would be greatly prejudiced if not entirely destroyed. . . . I have . . . laid the matter fully before Pierce & Bacon of Boston, who are willing to aid us to the extent of $100,000.00. . . . This house hold[s] ninety-five thousand of our paper, $75,000.00 of which matures after Jan. extending into April, thus increasing the firm's obligations to them to $175,000.00. . . . Mr. Soutter . . . undertakes to loan our Co. on his own account one hundred thousand . . . and frankly stated to me that if he had been at his bank for the last month and had the sum of money would cheerfully undertake to do the whole amount required. . . . These two accom[mo]dations are conditional that St. Louis or the west loan us the further sum of $200,000.00, which will put us all in good shape and enable us to go through. . . . See the banks and private bankers who hold R. M. and W. paper to meet at an early hour Tuesday to consider the proposition. If entertained we shall require $75,000.00 remitted by Tuesday or Wednesday, $50,000.00 by the tenth proximo, $40,000.00 by the 20th, and $35,000.00 by the 10th Nov.

On October 11 he forwarded a copy of this long letter to Waddell with the remark that if he succeeded in raising the money they could go on with their former good credit. Evidently he got the money he asked for and did go on, but not for long. Nothing could save Russell, Majors & Waddell now. During August and September he received $160,943.84 from the War Department as pay for transportation. Between October 1 and 11 he wrote $150,000.00 in acceptances upon Secretary Floyd and from the 11th to the 13th $120,000.00 more. During August, September, and October his receipts, from bonds given him by Bailey, pay for transportation from the War Department, acceptances written upon Secretary Floyd, and those as a result of his letter to Samuel & Allen, were, with a liberal discount allowed on both bonds and acceptances, in excess of $700,000. This was exclusive of receipts for mail, express, and passenger services on the Central Overland California & Pike's Peak Express Company's line. Huge though this sum was, it was not sufficient. To further complicate the situation, a near panic hit Wall Street, securities of all kinds sagged heavily, outstanding acceptances were being protested, and it was increasingly difficult to dispose of new ones. In addition, creditors with whom Russell had deposited bonds as security for loans were demanding additional margins and threatening to sell them in the open market if he did not comply with their request.

Long before Russell admitted defeat in his letter to Samuel & Allen, Alexander Majors saw what was coming. On October 17, 1860, he gave a deed of trust to Alexander W. Street for the benefit of persons to whom he or the firm of Russell, Majors & Waddell, or the Central Overland California & Pike's Peak Express Company were indebted. The liabilities he listed amounted to $37,167.56. Assets conveyed included some 2600 acres of land in Jackson County, Missouri, and Johnson County, Kansas; eighty-five lots in Shawnee, Kansas, forty lots in Olathe, same state; his interest in lands belonging to the West Kansas City Company, of which he was a stockholder; nine slaves; mules, horses, cattle, farming tools, wagons, etc., on the Jackson County farms. Two days later he gave another deed of trust to the same trustee for the benefit of other persons or firms whose claims upon him were listed at $38,373.18. Under these deeds of trust, which listed separate beneficiaries, his total liabilities amounted to $75,540.74. Most of them were Western concerns or residents although a few Eastern ones were mentioned.[160]

On October 31, Russell, Majors and Waddell addressed a personal letter to Jerome B. Simpson in which they pledged their sacred honor that in the event their firm failed they would give him the preference over all other general creditors. Neither Russell nor Waddell mentioned him in their later deeds of trust. Majors, however, acknowledged a debt of $5,000 on account of his having endorsed a Russell, Majors & Waddell acceptance for that amount.

Some time in the latter part of November, Russell went back to Washington to see Godard Bailey again. The tale he unfolded was far more doleful than it had been before. There was no hope of recovering

[160] Majors, Deed of Trust, Oct. 19, 1860.

the bonds he had hypothecated, he had no money with which to pay loans or increase margins, and their holders were about to sell them. "As a last forlorn hope," he said, "I determined to throw all the bonds upon the market, and even obtain and sell others, with the view of providing the means wherewith, in connection with other resources, to repurchase the whole, when they reached the lowest market price." [161]

Russell was now a badly frightened man, frantically grasping at intangibles. $350,000 in additional bonds, he assured Bailey, would protect Secretary Floyd's acceptances, restore Russell, Majors & Waddell's credit, enable him to repurchase and replace bonds previously taken, and enable the firm to carry out its contracts. Being already hopelessly bogged down in trouble, Bailey agreed to Russell's proposal on condition that an amount of Secretary Floyd's acceptances equal to the face value of all the bonds be deposited with him. This being agreed upon Bailey delivered $333,000 worth of Missouri and Tennessee issues to him, making a total of $870,000. Russell deposited $735,000 worth of the agreed acceptances with him at that time and $135,000 later. In addition he gave Bailey a Russell, Majors & Waddell receipt for the full amount. [162]

Not long after these bonds were delivered to Russell, Godard Bailey saw the hopelessness of the situation in which he was involved. On December 1 he wrote a letter to Secretary of the Interior Jacob Thompson confessing the whole transaction and listing the stolen securities. He also declared that his motive was unselfish, that he did not use the bonds for his own purposes, and that no officer of the Government had advised him to do what he had done. On the 13th he gave this letter to Charles G. Wagner, a relative and a former employee of the Department of the Interior, with a request that it be delivered to Secretary Thompson five days before the expiration of his term of office. Wagner, thinking that it contained information concerning Bailey's resignation, made a memorandum upon the envelope and tossed it into his desk. [163]

About this time Bailey also called upon Senator H. M. Rice of Minnesota and told him what he had done. Rice advised him to lay the facts before Secretaries Thompson and Floyd. Soon afterward Bailey told him he had done this.

---

161 Russell, "Statement," Mar. 28, 1861.
162 *H.R.*, 36th Cong., 2d sess., Report 78, pp. 29, 277.
163 *Ibid.*, p. 258. Russell, "Statement," Mar. 28, 1861.

On December 20, Bailey again called at Wagner's office and, not finding him in, left a note instructing him to deliver the letter to Secretary Thompson immediately upon his return from North Carolina. "It concerns my honor," he said, "that Mr. Thompson should receive that letter at the earliest possible moment." Greatly disturbed by this statement, Wagner hurried to Bailey's home immediately after the evening meal and demanded an explanation. To his consternation Bailey, in the presence of his wife, confessed the whole transaction with Russell and again requested that the letter be delivered to Secretary Thompson at once. Next day Wagner went to the Secretary's office but he had not yet returned.[164]

Having decided to fully disclose the whole affair, Bailey made up a package of the acceptances and the receipt, addressed it to Secretary Thompson, and took it to the home of Senator Rice on December 22. Not finding the Senator at home he left it, together with a note instructing him to deliver it to the Secretary. Rice read the note when he returned, became greatly alarmed about the matter, and hurried to Bailey's house. Here he found Charles G. Wagner, who was on his way to deliver Bailey's letter of December 1 to Secretary Thompson. The Senator informed Bailey that if the package had anything to do with the bonds he did not wish to keep it in his possession. When Bailey admitted that it did he asked permission to deliver it to President Buchanan at once. Bailey consented to this proposal, Wagner gave Rice the letter Bailey had written December 1, and the Senator went away. He delivered the package and the letter to President Buchanan. While they were discussing the matter, Secretary of State Jeremiah S. Black and Attorney General Edwin M. Stanton came in. Presently Secretary Thompson, who had returned sooner than was expected, also arrived.[165]

After a discussion as to the proper course to pursue, it was decided that they should first go to the Department of the Interior and check the bonds in the Indian Trust Fund to see whether more than those mentioned in the receipt for $870,000 were missing. Senator Rice went to Bailey's home, got the key to the safe where the securities were kept, and returned to the White House. At Thompson's request, Stanton and Black went to the Department of the Interior while Thompson and Wag-

---

[164] *H.R.,* 36th Cong., 2d sess., Report 78, p. 258.
[165] *Ibid.,* pp. 357, 376.

ner drove to Bailey's home to ask him to go with them. He readily consented to this and assisted them in checking the bond account. All of them were there except those he had given to Russell. Next morning Thompson had warrants issued for the arrest of Russell and Bailey.[166]

This affair, coming as it did in the twilight of President Buchanan's stormy administration, shook the ground under his feet. Hastily calling a meeting of the Cabinet on Sunday evening, December 23, they questioned Bailey until morning. He said he made a favorable impression upon the members and that they were disposed to sympathize with him until he refused to disclose the name of the person who informed him Secretary Floyd's position would be jeopardized in the event the acceptances were protested. When he persisted in keeping his secret, whatever sympathy they may have felt for him was turned to prejudice. Within the next day or so he was arrested and put in prison.[167]

The relation of Secretary Floyd to the bond transaction, apart from having signed the acceptances Russell deposited with Bailey, is obscure and mystifying. Robert W. Latham testified before the Select Committee that on the evening of December 20 he had an interview with Secretary Floyd, who referred to the stolen bonds and inquired whether Bailey had trust funds of any kind in his possession which could have been turned over to Russell. That was two days before Bailey's confession was handed to President Buchanan. This would confirm Bailey's statement to Senator Rice that he had told Floyd about the matter. When Latham called upon Floyd on the evening of December 21 and told him he was going to New York the next day, the Secretary asked him to see Russell, tell him a serious difficulty relating to the bonds had arisen, and persuade him to return to Washington at once. That morning Floyd instructed W. R. Drinkard to telegraph Russell that it was vitally important that he should meet Latham, who was traveling on the Amboy boat, at Pier No. 1.[168]

There can be no question that Secretary Floyd was in full possession of all the essential details of the affair at least twenty-four hours before Bailey's confession was placed in President Buchanan's hands, with the possible exception of the deposit of the acceptances. Knowledge of that angle of it was of minor importance. He resigned his post in the Cabinet

166 *Ibid.*, pp. 357, 358.
167 *Ibid.*, p. 68.
168 *Ibid.*, p. 126.

on December 29th by request of the President. Two days later he testified before the Select Committee regarding the acceptances, but the stolen bonds were not mentioned. Not long afterward he moved his family to Virginia. On January 25, 1861, he was indicted by a District of Columbia grand jury for malversation in office. He returned to Washington, gave bail, and demanded trial. On March 11, 1861, the United States Attorney dismissed the case for lack of proof to sustain the charge and a *nolle prosequi* was entered.[169]

Russell met Latham at Pier No. 1 in New York, but the subject of their conversation is not recorded. On Monday morning, December 24, Latham went to Russell's office to ask him when he was going to Washington. Not long after Latham's arrival officers came in, arrested Russell, and took him to Washington. He was put in jail and his bond fixed at $500,000, a sum which he said "exceeded anything ever known in the annals of judicial proceedings in any part of the world." Russell's friends from the West immediately underwrote his bond, but because they were nonresidents their offer was rejected. Residents of the District of Columbia had to put up $300,000 of the required amount. When the full amount could not be secured, he was compelled to remain in jail until the bond was reduced.[170]

In his public statement written for the newspapers, Russell said his plan to repurchase the abstracted securities on a depressed market was wrecked by Bailey's confession. The implication was that had this not happened he would have succeeded. No proof, however, was offered to show that he had sufficient funds with which to accomplish this design. On the contrary, evidence that he did not have it is rather voluminous. His affairs were so complicated and involved at this time and actual records so limited that only the broadest of general conclusions can be reached. It is clear, however, that he was hopelessly bankrupt, overwhelmed with debt, and totally disgraced.

On December 31, 1860, Russell made the first move to protect his many creditors, one of whom was James N. Simpson of New York, to whom he was indebted for $61,850. A deed of trust was drawn up in which the debt was acknowledged and a penal bond of $100,000, condi-

---

[169] James Ford Rhodes, *History of the United States,* pp. 236-238. *Record,* U.S. District Courts, District of Columbia, March 1861, Criminal Trials No. 33.

[170] *H.R.,* 36th Cong., 2d sess., Report 78, p. 227. Russell, Statement, Mar. 28, 1861.

tioned upon the payment of the debt, was included. It was intended to make Simpson the beneficiary and Benjamin Holladay the trustee, but the draftsman who wrote it inadvertently erred and reversed their positions in the instrument. Without noticing this error the three signed it. Under this deed some four thousand acres of land in Lafayette and Johnson Counties, Missouri, were listed. The error was not discovered by Simpson until his counsel in Missouri notified him of it. For some reason, possibly because of the Civil War, nothing was done about it until March 7, 1868. On that date Simpson filed suit in the Lafayette County Court against Russell, Holladay, and others to rectify the mistake. In the meantime a part of the land had been sold to innocent parties. The case dragged along and was at length begun in Liberty, Missouri, in March, 1870. Before it was concluded Russell died. Simpson finally got judgment for $105,948.44.[171]

[171] Russell, Deed of trust to James N. Simpson, Dec. 31, 1860. Simpson, Petition against Russell, *et al.*, Mar. 7, 1868.

XIII

THE BOND SCANDAL (CONTINUED)

ON DECEMBER 24, 1860, Representative John Sherman of Ohio, at the request of Secretary Thompson, introduced a resolution in the House calling for a Select Committee to investigate the matter relating to the abstracted bonds. It held its first hearing on December 27 and completed its work February 8, 1861. A total of forty-six witnesses were examined. Their testimony, considered as a whole, is as enlightening and valuable as one could expect from the nature of the proceedings. In analyzing and weighing it, one must constantly remind himself that he is not dealing with the record of a court of justice.

Some of the witnesses were frightened, others belligerent and resentful, and a few slippery. Most of them, however, being anxious to tell what they knew, were truthful in their statements. Some seemed afflicted with a pronounced loss of memory where important facts and dates were concerned. Since in the main, general information was sought, that was the kind obtained. From the very beginning two principal objects seemed to govern the hearings: to investigate Secretary Floyd's acceptances, and to find the abstracted bonds. The first endeavor was quite successful but the latter only partially so.

Three of Russell's friends testified, Luke Lea, Luther R. Smoot, and Robert W. Latham, all of whom made a rather poor showing. The report of the Committee branded Lea as "artful and unwilling." Obviously he was more than that—he was thoroughly alarmed lest he be implicated in the affair. Since the case was not tried in court his actual relation to it was not fully revealed. Judging by his and Russell's testimony alone, however, it would have borne investigation. Smoot's straightforward testimony was given without effort to shield anybody or conceal anything. He was not haunted by fears of any kind. What he said neither helped nor hindered Russell.

The most difficult witness of them all was Robert W. Latham. He stated that his business in Washington was to act as agent for anybody who chose to employ him. For several years he had worked for John B. Floyd, up to 1859. He kept only random memoranda of his transactions, he said. Therefore he exhibited an extremely poor memory concerning certain important matters. Knowing his rights he stood solidly upon them. He also apparently knew a great deal about certain angles relating to Floyd's acceptances but refused to tell anything. It is evident that the Committee suspected Floyd of having personally profited from Russell, Majors & Waddell's contracts and that Latham was the go-between. To every question designed to elicit information on that point he invariably replied, "I decline to answer." Consequently his testimony was very damaging to himself, Floyd, and Russell, in that he left the impression there was some secret arrangement between the latter. In all the material of the Waddell Collection, there is nothing in the way of *direct, conclusive* evidence that Floyd received money from Russell but there is much to arouse suspicion that he did.

Judging solely by Russell's letters to Waddell, one is forced to conclude that influence, favoritism, and possibly other factors which were never meant to receive publicity were involved in the Russell, Majors & Waddell contracts. Below are some of the passages bearing upon the subject:

[March 20, 1858] Mr. Majors starts tonight. You must not say a word to him about what I wrote you yesterday. All will go right. You need have no fear. Secretary of War has promised us all we want, tho he cannot change the contract.

[New York, April 12, 1859] I have already obtained from the Department $125,000.00 that no other living man could have carried, and I think I will be able to get half as much more out of matters that you are not dreaming of. . . .

[Not dated] Secretary of War and Quartermaster General are strong friend in the matter as also all the clerks and assistant quartermasters in this Department.

[New York, August 19, 1859] I am really astonished and mortified at your conclusions with regard to the results of my visit to Washington. I had flattered myself that I had been of some service to the concern. Knowing as I do that my course there has secured to us all the advantages we have enjoyed the past two years. And that what I have secured in outside things, which I well know would have been lost, had I not pursued the course I did, and which has amounted to largely more than I have expended or given away, not only so through the influence brought to bear in this way we have obtained much work and many favors that otherwise would have been cut off. I will only refer to one. How could we have gotten along without Gov't accept[ances?] . . . . That was never done before and I carried it in the face of opposition of the Q.M. General Dep't. However this is only one of dozen important things secured and having done as I thought well and for the best I feel much mortified to hear the recipient of my sacrificing labor complain and say it would have been better had I never visited Washington.

Godard Bailey, out of prison on a $5,000 bond, did not appear before the Select Committee. Being under criminal prosecution he could not be compelled to appear. After all, his full confession was filed with the Committee by Secretary Thompson. About this time he was reported as saying that Russell knew nothing about the ownership of the abstracted bonds when the first $150,000 was delivered to him. Secretary Thompson was also quoted as saying the same thing. Bailey was arraigned in the March 1861 term of the District of Columbia Criminal Court on a charge of larceny, abstracting bonds, and conspiracy to cheat the United States government, to all of which he pleaded not guilty. The case lay dormant until September, 1862, when it was called up for trial. Bailey not appearing, his bond was declared forfeit. In June, 1869, it was again called up and a *nolle prosequi* entered by the United States Attorney. This ended the case.[172]

Russell voluntarily appeared before the Select Committee on January 14, 1861. He, too, could have declined to come had he chosen to do so. When Chairman Morris informed him that since he was under criminal prosecution he would not be required to answer any questions, he replied, "I am anxious to make a full statement in regard to the bonds. I claim to be an honest man, and would prefer to make out a statement of the whole transaction in writing and have it spread on your records."[173]

If the Committee preferred, however, he would make it verbally. Then he was sworn and the hearing began. After a brief interrogation concerning the disposal of the bonds, Russell renewed his request for time to make a written statement. This was granted, with as much time for it as he desired.

[172] *Record*, District Court, District of Columbia, Criminal Sci. Fa. No. 1, March Term, 1861.
[173] *H.R.*, 36th Cong., 2d sess., Report 78, p. 232.

THE BOND SCANDAL (CONTINUED)

Four days later he reappeared with the statement, dated January 16, 1861, which was prepared by himself and his attorneys. Among them was Thomas P. Akers, fellow Lexingtonian, former pastor of the Methodist Episcopal Church there, member of the 34th Congress, orator and financier. This time Russell was questioned at length. The members of the Committee were courteous and in the majority of his answers Russell was frankly honest. Occasionally they were obscure and unsatisfactory. He unhesitatingly admitted securing and disposing of the Indian Trust Fund bonds but was not very helpful, probably because of lack of definite information, in locating them. For a man under criminal prosecution and not compelled to testify at all, he was, in his testimony, which fills twenty-five pages in the Committee Report, amazingly frank. When asked, "did you ever, directly or indirectly, pay any person any consideration, or make any person a present, for services rendered to you connected with your business with the War Department?" he declined to answer and asked permission to consult his counsel. This was granted.[174]

On January 23 he again appeared. After being reminded that he was not compelled to testify, the Chairman informed him that the examination might be waived and, if he so desired, any or all of the testimony previously given would be stricken from the record. In order that he might be more fully informed as to his rights the Chairman gave him a copy of the Act of Congress governing such proceedings and asked him if he understood it. He replied that he did but wished until the next day to confer with counsel, which was granted.[175]

The result of this conference was a statement to the effect that the question concerning payment to persons for assistance in conducting his business with the War Department was not pertinent to the subject under investigation. Previous to that Thomas P. Akers had a conversation with Chairman Morris in which he said that Russell had no desire to withhold the answer providing the Committee would obtain authority from the House of Representatives to ask it. He also stated that Russell wished to "make a clean breast" of the whole matter. On January 25 he came back with his statement in his pocket. Before undertaking to answer questions he asked that he be allowed the presence of counsel to advise him from

174 *Ibid.*, pp. 263-288, 333.
175 *Ibid.*, pp. 290-291.

time to time. In reply Chairman Morris informed him that the only question the Committee wished him to answer was whether he desired the testimony he had already given to become a part of its report or be stricken out. In reply Russell stated that he was willing for the examination to proceed but desired the presence of counsel. He then handed in his statement and left. That was his last appearance before the Committee. On January 29 he, together with Floyd and Bailey, were indicted by a District of Columbia grand jury.[176]

On February 27 the House passed a resolution authorizing the Committee to question him regarding payment for services rendered in connection with the War Department. The resolution concerning Russell's relations with government officials was the fruit of a long standing suspicion that Secretary Floyd profited personally from contracts given to Russell, Majors & Waddell. On the day it was passed the Chairman of the Committee telegraphed ex-Secretary Floyd, who was at Abingdon, Virginia, that the examination of witnesses under this new authority would begin the next day and that if he should be implicated he would be allowed to be present at the hearings. He made no reply to this message.[177]

Immediately after appearing before the Committee for the last time on January 25, Russell went to New York. On the day following the passage of the new resolution Chairman Morris telegraphed him at his office requesting him to return to Washington. Alfred Lockwood, an employee, received it and replied that Russell had not come in yet but that he would attempt to reach him. With the passage of this resolution his status before the Committee had materially changed. Since he was not under criminal prosecution for dealings with government officials, he enjoyed no immunity from questioning upon that subject. After waiting three days for him to appear Chairman Morris instructed United States Marshal Isaiah Rynders of New York to find him and bring him to the capital. On March 2 Rynders telegraphed back that he had been searching for him but could not find him. It was rumored, he said, that Russell was in Philadelphia but he did not believe it. That day Joseph A. Monheimer, partner in the Central Overland California & Pike's Peak Express Company, testified before the Committee that he had that morning received

---

[176] *H.R.*, 36th Cong., 2d sess., Report 78, pp. 294, 362, 363.
[177] *Ibid.*, pp. 353, 354, 355.

a letter from his brother, Asher, in New York with a note from Russell enclosed.[178]

Obviously Russell had changed his mind about making a clean breast of the whole business and was hiding somewhere in New York. The Committee concluded that his failure to appear was due to influence by other persons. No doubt they were right. If he had paid money to an officer of the Government in return for favors he was subject to prosecution. His hiding out and failure to make a clean breast of the matter inevitably arouses suspicion that he feared another indictment against him.

Two days after Russell's arrest, Thomas P. Akers wrote Waddell a long letter in which he exonerated him in the affair concerning the bonds and laid the blame for it all at Secretary Floyd's door.

It is firmly believed that Floyd sent Bailey to Mr. Russell in the first instance for the purpose of getting his absolute acceptances taken up so that he might replace them with conditional ones. . . . It is further believed that Bailey acted under a promise of a pardon and the course of the prosecution sustains this view of the case. . . . It is sufficient to say that this act of flagrant injustice has been traced to the President who seeks to screen the deformities of a rotten and fallen administration by offering up Mr. Russell as a victim of popular clamor. . . . In a word if it were possible to drag to light the doings of the administration the evidence would be as clear as noonday that the President and his pliant Cabinet ministers have deliberately spread their meshes to entangle and victimize Mr. Russell.[179]

Russell's friends naturally did and thought everything they could in his favor. The idea that he had been lured into a trap by Secretary Floyd and the administration gained such currency that H. H. Bancroft took cognizance of it when he wrote his *Chronicles of the Builders*. He said that,

. . . . Russell . . . . fell into a difficulty, if indeed, it were not a trap set for him by the friends of the Southern Route. . . . He was induced to take $830,000.00 in bonds of the Interior Department, as a loan, and giving as security acceptances on the War Department furnished him by Secretary Floyd, a part of which were not yet due.[180]

[178] *Ibid.*, pp. 354, 355, 362.   [179] Thomas P. Akers to Waddell, Dec. 26, 1860.

[180] H. H. Bancroft, *Chronicles of the Builders*, II, 323—quoted by Victor M. Berthold, "William H. Russell, Originator and Developer of the Famous Pony Express," *Collector's Club Philatelist*, VII, 18; see also, *Liberty Tribune*, April 12, 1861.

The truth is nobody set a trap for Russell. Never a word to that effect did he utter himself. Neither he, nor Luke Lea, nor W. R. Drinkard, all of whom knew exactly how the first transaction involving $150,000 worth of bonds originated, gave a very satisfactory account of it. He does say that he "consented" to take the second lot of $387,000. It must be remembered that he was at that time aware of their ownership and of the fact that he was deliberately participating in an embezzlement of great proportions.

In January 1861, Russell's case came up in the Criminal Court of the District of Columbia. His attorney pleaded that since he had already been examined upon the same subject by the Select Committee of the House he should be allowed to go free. The Court adopted this view and quashed the indictment against him.[181] This is not to be interpreted as exoneration or acquittal, for the fact that he had received stolen property and appropriated it to his own private purposes remained. Freedom from prosecution under a technicality in nowise affected his moral responsibility.

On March 20, Russell wrote Waddell from his New York office that he was detained there making up his public statement. That statement, which was published in the newspapers over his signature, is a remarkable document, most of which is devoted to an obvious bid for sympathy on the ground that the government owed Russell, Majors & Waddell a huge sum of money. Reduced to various items it read as follows:

For freights withheld in 1857	$ 655,550
For interest three years, at 12 percent actually paid by the firm	235,998
For losses in 1857 train	300,000
For interest on same, three years	108,000
For freights withheld by Government for 1860–61	50,000
	$1,349,548 [182]

In this statement he bitterly declaimed against the Select Committee and its report for stating, as he alleged, that $6,137,395 worth of acceptances were outstanding. Charging that Russell's statements were ram-

181 *Record*, U.S. District Courts, District of Columbia, Criminal Trials No. 33, Minutes, 1861.
182 Russell, "Statement," Mar. 28, 1861.

bling, vague, and unsatisfactory upon this point, the Committee had based its estimate upon the records furnished by the War Department. Here again it was handicapped, for the only record of acceptances was kept by Richard B. Irwin upon loose slips of paper. According to these, it reported, $5,339,395 worth were still in circulation. This was said, not to discredit Russell, but to show that the handling of these acceptances by that Department was careless and inaccurate. Russell's figures indicated that all issued previous to 1860 had been retired, that $2,118,000 had been secured in that year, of which only $613,000 were outstanding. The best evidence as to the amount is the sworn statement of John Perry Sellar of Leavenworth, Kansas, clerk of the trustees of Russell, Majors & Waddell. On February 1, 1862, he listed $861,000 as outstanding and unpaid. This did not include the $870,000 deposited with Godard Bailey. When that amount is added the total is $1,731,000.[183]

On January 30, 1861, Russell made another deed of trust by his attorney, Elbridge Burden, of Lexington, Missouri, to Eugene B. Allen, of the firm of Samuel & Allen, as trustee for the benefit of Benjamin Holladay. This deed covered about the same property as the first, was subject to it, and was an effort to protect Holladay for money advanced to Russell, Majors & Waddell and the Central Overland California & Pike's Peak Express Company.[184]

Still another deed of trust was made to Allen on the same day for the benefit of concerns and individuals, mostly in Lexington, to whom he owed $46,664.05. Some six thousand acres of land, which were included in the Simpson-Holladay instrument, were set aside for the benefit of creditors.[185] By the giving of these three deeds of trust he stripped himself of most of his empire. All that remained to him was his interest in the freighting firm, the Central Overland California & Pike's Peak Express Company, the R. B. Bradford & Company store in Denver, the Majors & Russell store in Leavenworth, the Waddell & Russell store in Lexington, and some property in Denver. These were all so inextricably bound up with the fortunes of Russell, Majors & Waddell and so heavily involved on their own account that they were more of a liability than an asset. His ruin was now complete. The good name he had built up

183 Charles B. Goodrich, *Opinion*, etc., p. 18.
184 Russell, Deed of trust to Allen, Jan. 30, 1861.
185 Russell, Deed of trust to Allen, Jan. 30, 1861.

for himself was clouded and his honor, which he had said was dearer to him than life itself, was stained.

Out in the West his partners moved swiftly in the face of overwhelming disaster. From January 23 to February 1, 1861, Waddell gave five deeds of trust to his son John W. and to Elbridge Burden for the benefit of various concerns and persons in Lexington, St. Louis, and other places to whom he owed $52,607. Included in his list of assets was everything he owned, such as lands in Lafayette, Carroll, Ray, and DeKalb Counties, Missouri, his home in Lexington, town lots, household goods of all kinds, farming tools, hogs, cattle, mules, horses, carriages, wagons, harness, ox-yokes, chains, etc. Some of the beneficiaries were personal creditors while others held obligations of R. B. Bradford & Company, Waddell & Russell, and Russell, Majors & Waddell. No mention is made of Secretary Floyd's acceptances but doubtless some of the creditors held them. Like Russell, Waddell stripped himself of his possessions. Waddell family tradition says that Mrs. Waddell, because of distrust of Russell, had previously caused him to set aside $100,000 in her name. Something like this was certainly done, for on February 1, 1861, Bradford wrote him that Alexander Majors and his Denver agent, A. Byram, were publicly saying that Waddell had taken $50,000 from the firm of Russell, Majors & Waddell and appropriated it to the benefit of his children.[186]

Alexander Majors also met disaster with more deeds of trust and assignments. On January 25, 1861, he filed with the Recorder of Deeds of Jackson County, Missouri, a list of assets and liabilities which were to be considered a part of the deed of trust to Alexander W. Street on October 17, 1860. The former consisted of bills receivable and notes amounting to $53,845.71. In addition he included 1,500 head of oxen at "Pike's Peak" (Denver), Arkansas Grazing and Mining Country, and in the Raton Mountains, seventy-five wagons, some in Jackson County and others at Fort Wise on the Arkansas River, others at Bluff Spring station, all camp and train equipment, 3,000 sacks of flour at Bluff Spring, dry goods and groceries at the same place, ninety mules on one of the Jackson County farms, about 1,001 head of oxen in Kansas Territory, one hundred head at Council Grove, Kansas Territory, thirty-one rifles and revolvers, buggies, mules, harness, and camp equipage at Kansas City, on the Arkansas River, furnishings for his home at Nebraska City, and

[186] Waddell, Deeds of trust, Jan. 23, 30, Feb. 1, 1861. Bradford to Waddell, Feb. 1, 1861.

other items. His schedule of liabilities amounted to $82,286.25, which included most of his debts listed in the previous deed of trust. With this latter one he undertook to protect both his creditors and employees, clerks, wagon masters, and bullwhackers.[187]

Thinking there might be something left over when the obligations mentioned in the first two deeds of trust were satisfied, he made another on January 26, 1861, providing that any sum remaining should be applied to the indebtedness of Russell, Majors & Waddell. In order that this might be properly done he listed such of the firm's liabilities as were known to him. The total was $446,069.11, of which sum $368,544.73 was for drafts drawn by Jones, Russell & Company and endorsed by Russell, Majors & Waddell, John S. Jones, and Samuel & Allen. The remainder, $117,524.38 consisted of drafts drawn by or upon Jones, Russell & Company, Russell, Majors & Waddell, and endorsed by Smoot & Russell, Samuel & Allen or others. Of this amount $15,000 was for Secretary Floyd's acceptances.[188]

One reason for Russell's letter to Samuel & Allen of September was that they had endorsed a major portion of the drafts. The total liabilities listed by Russell and his partners was $500,526.15. Great though this sum was it fell far short of representing their full obligations. To this must be added the $861,000 of unpaid acceptances listed by John Perry Sellar, less $15,000 acknowledged by Majors, which left $836,000 outstanding. This, added to what was listed in their various deeds of trust, raised their indebtedness to the large sum of $1,331,526.13. Since neither Russell nor Waddell evaluated the assets upon which they gave deeds of trust it is impossible to arrive at any estimate of them. It is obvious, however, that they fell far short of balancing their liabilities.

With the making of these assignments, Alexander Majors ended his career as government freighter, stage coach operator, and financier. They also apparently terminated relationship and contact with his partners of the glory days. So far as the record is concerned they never met again. Skimpy though Majors' account of it all is, one cannot help reading criticism and a restrained spirit of recrimination between the lines.

At forty-six years of age and under radically different conditions he faced the exceedingly hard task of beginning all over again. He continued to make his home in Nebraska City and managed to get enough

187 Majors, Deed of trust to Alexander Street, Jan. 25, 1861.
188 Majors, Deed of trust to Finis B. Ewing and Eugene B. Allen, Feb. 26, 1861.

oxen, bullwhackers, and wagons together to continue in the business of private freighting. In the summer of 1865 he sent two trains to Salt Lake City. Instead of returning them to the Missouri River he forwarded one to Boise, Idaho, and the other to Helena, Montana. This was a mistake, for both trains ran into trouble. The one for Idaho was smothered by a severe snowstorm and had to lay over until spring. Every ox in it froze to death. In later years, when the railroad ran that way, trains were halted at the spot that the passengers might alight and view the pathetic pile of bones. The train for Montana fared better. When the wagon master ran into a heavy snowstorm at Beaverhead Pass, he parked the wagons, unyoked the oxen, and drove them to Beaverhead Valley, where they spent the winter. When spring came they were driven out again and the wagons moved to their destination.[189]

In the spring of 1866, Majors set out from Nebraska City for Helena, Montana, by way of Denver and Salt Lake City, to look after the stalled train. Thirty days were required for the journey. Accompanied by his eldest son, Greene, he visited Brigham Young in Salt Lake City. When the business concerning the train was concluded at Helena, it was sent east to Fort Union on the Missouri River, to which his youngest son, Benjamin, had brought a consignment of goods by steamboat. Majors himself and Greene accompanied the train. After loading it for the return journey to Helena, he turned it over to his sons and returned to Nebraska City. In the spring of 1867, he sold the entire train to Edward Creighton, builder of the east section of the transcontinental telegraph line six years before.[190]

In the fall of 1867, Majors moved his family from Nebraska City to Salt Lake City, Utah. Before he left, the citizens of the place presented him with a gold watch and chain as a token of the esteem in which they held him. Out in Utah he engaged in the work of grading the railroad bed and furnishing ties and telegraph poles for the Union Pacific Railroad. On May 10, 1869, the western and eastern divisions met at Promontory, Utah, where a gold spike was driven into a tie by Leland Stanford. Majors and his son, Benjamin, saw it all and heard the fulsome speeches delivered on that occasion. In that incident there was much of pathos for the completion of the transcontinental railroad marked the end of an

---

[189] Hildegarde Hawthorne, *Ox-team Miracle*, pp. 224-226.
[190] *Ibid.*, pp. 226-231. Majors, *Seventy Years on the Frontier*, pp. 221-227.

era in which he had played a conspicuous part. Concerning it he said, "My calling as a freighter and overland stager having been deposed by the building of the telegraph lines and the completion of the transcontinental railway, I was compelled to look for a new industry."[191]

The new industry he fixed upon was that of prospecting for silver in the Raft River Mountains of northwestern Utah, some twenty-five miles from the little town of Kelton. This proving a failure he went back home, joined a man by the name of R. C. Chambers, and prospected the Wasatch Mountains some twenty or twenty-five miles southeast of Salt Lake City. After 1879 he made his home in various places. He visited St. Louis in 1886 and stood upon the bank of the Mississippi River where he had landed from the ferry boat in 1818, sixty-seven years before. From 1887 to 1890 or 1891 he made his home in Denver. There William F. (Buffalo Bill) Cody found him living all alone in a little cabin with scarcely enough to eat. He was writing the story of his life on the frontier and on the Plains, with the pathetic hope that it would turn out a financial success. The floor was covered with manuscript. Buffalo Bill looked at it, decided it was worth while, urged him to complete it, and promised to pay for printing it when it was finished. After a year in Europe with his Wild West show he returned. Finding the manuscript completed he gave it to Prentiss Ingraham, who was to edit it. Majors complained that Ingraham tried to make him exaggerate and Ingraham said that Majors was too modest. The book was printed in 1893,[192] but it is doubtful that it so much as paid for its publication. The major portion of it is devoted to dull, uninteresting chapters on Missouri, the Mormons, dogs, beaver, buffalo, the brown bear, Doniphan's Expedition to Mexico, 1846-47, Kit Carson, etc., with only minor attention to himself, his family, his partners, the freighting and staging business, and other matters of vital importance.

It is said that after the book was out, Buffalo Bill took him to his ranch in Nebraska. On August 13, 1896, the citizens of Nebraska City held a celebration and invited Majors, Buffalo Bill, Edward Creighton, and other notables as guests. Majors delivered an address, in which he told the story of how he had employed the lad "Billy" Cody and paid him a man's wages of twenty-five dollars per month. In 1899 he attended

---

[191] Majors, *op. cit.,* p. 267.

[192] *Ibid.,* pp. 17, 267. Frank Wornall, Statement to the author. *Kansas City Star,* Jan. 15, 1900.

the Second Annual Convention of the National Livestock Association in Denver, January 24-27. As usual, when he appeared in public, he was called upon to make a few remarks. Less than a year later he went to Chicago on business. There he contracted pneumonia and died on January 14, 1900, in his eighty-sixth year, with a grandson and a granddaughter at his bedside. He was buried in Union Cemetery, Kansas City, Missouri, with fifteen persons present.

Alexander Majors was truly a remarkable man in many respects. His eighty-six years spanned the most critical period in American history. Born ten years after the Louisiana Purchase and only eight after the return of Lewis and Clark from their memorable expedition, he not only lived to see the national boundary moved westward to the Pacific Coast but did much to place it there. He was fifteen years old when the first locomotive, one brought from England, moved upon American soil, yet thirty years before his death he stood by and watched the driving of the golden spike which symbolized the opening of railway traffic from the Atlantic to the Pacific. As a boy in western Missouri he listened with rapt attention to the marvelous tales of hunters and trappers concerning the Rocky Mountains, far away across the wide, mysterious plains. Before his career as freighter ended, he had crossed those plains scores of times and his wagons had rumbled through those mountains, from Old Mexico to Canada. When he was born, the British and American forces under General Andrew Jackson were maneuvering for the decisive Battle of New Orleans. He died while the echoes of the Spanish-American War were still reverberating through the world and only fourteen years before the outbreak of World War I.

XIV
RUIN

ONE OF THE FACTORS which may have contributed to the quashing of the indictment against Russell was talk in Congress about the appointment of a Commission to adjudicate the question of his claims, acceptances, and abstracted bonds. There was also talk about the possibility of the government bringing suit to recover the bonds. In a letter to Waddell from Washington on February 11, 1861, Russell expressed satisfaction with either proposition.

If the Government will sue us and in a court of equity and chancery, we can bring in our claims and assets, so that in either event we can pay through.

By this time his incurable, irrepressible sanguine nature had reasserted itself.

You talk as though you did not expect to pay through, [he chided]. I do, and feel entire confidence. . . . I can after the 20th get information of our mail pay for the Co. if the drafts are properly fixed and sent to me. . . . Have great faith in getting mail contract all right.

The mail contract Russell had great faith in getting was the one for carrying the mail over the Central Route from the Missouri River to California. Everything considered, his hopes of this were not unreasonable. The Pony Express was keeping that Route before the public and the myth that it could not be traveled in winter was forgotten. At the opening of Congress in December, 1860, its friends girded themselves for a final, victorious battle. On February 2, 1861, the Annual Post Route Bill was presented to the Senate. It provided for a daily mail from the Missouri River to California with pay not to exceed $800,000 per year. The Post Offices and Post Roads Committee of the same body was grappling with the problem of consolidating the Southern and Central Route lines. While these measures were being debated, word reached Washington and Congress that Butterfield's Overland Mail line had been "cut up by the roots" by Confederate forces and that all its stages had been stopped throughout Texas. With seven Southern states already seceded and others moving swiftly in that direction, California could not be neglected. Five days after the disturbing news of what had happened to Butterfield's line reached the capital, the Senate Finance Committee reported the Post Office Appropriation Bill. This provided for the bodily removal of that line from the Southern to the Central Route, a daily mail on a twenty-three-day schedule, the running of the Pony Express until the transcontinental telegraph line was completed, and pay of $1,150,000 per year.[193]

Senator Gwin supported the measure but thought that $1,000,000 was enough and argued that the Central Overland California & Pike's Peak Express Company should have an opportunity to bid for the contract. It was not fair, he said, to arbitrarily set aside the men who had started the Pony Express and kept it running. By mid-December Russell was discouraged, both by the outlook for the nation and the mail contract.

The condition of our country is awful [he wrote], how it will end God only knows. If in Civil War our friends think we are in a good position to meet it. If troubles are settled and confidence restored we can go on without trouble and wind up to great advantage. I really fear the worst. If anything is done will get a good mail contract at least to Denver City.

By this time he had apparently abandoned the idea of a line from the Missouri River to California because, as he said, "The whole line will require too much additional capital and we have it not." [194]

The Central Route was possibly due to triumph in this session of Congress, even without the catastrophe to the Butterfield line. It won, but Russell lost. Bankruptcy and involvement in the biggest scandal of the day imposed too great a handicap to his negotiations. Moreover, since the Post Office Department was already under contract with the Overland Mail Company the obvious course was to move what was left of it to the Central Route. In resorting to this plan, members of Congress and the Postmaster General were not without concern for the Central Overland California & Pike's Peak Express Company. While the debates were on, Senator Latham remarked that he understood an agreement had

[193] Hafen, *Overland Mail*, p. 210.
[194] Russell to Waddell, Dec. 16, 1860.

been reached whereby the Overland Mail Company was to take over the express company at an appraised price.[195] While this was not correct, it indicates there was some effort to be fair to all parties concerned.

Disappointed and discouraged though Russell was, he was not yet ready to give up the struggle. Since he had been defeated by the friends of the Southern Route and the Overland Mail Company, he swallowed his pride and joined them. On March 16, 1861, he signed two contracts, one with that company and the other with the Western Stage Company. The contract with the former provided that the Central Overland California & Pike's Peak Express Company should carry all mail and passengers, both through and local, from the Missouri River to Salt Lake City, and that the Overland Mail Company should carry them the remainder of the way to California. For this service Russell's company was to receive $470,000 per year for carrying the mail, after one-half the amount, for sea service, had been deducted. Receipts from through express and passenger service to California were to be divided equally between the two companies. Those from local business between the Missouri River and Salt Lake City were divided on a 70-30 percent basis, with the larger portion going to the Central Overland California & Pike's Peak Express Company. Receipts from the Pony Express were to be divided equally, with each paying all expenses on its own portion of the line. A general superintendent, appointed by the Overland Mail Company, and paid by both, was to have general charge and supervision of the whole line but with no authority to interfere in the management of the eastern division, between the Missouri River and Salt Lake City. An agent stationed at Fort Kearny was to be paid by both companies. The Overland Mail Company reserved the right to make an exclusive contract with Wells, Fargo & Company for all express business going east from any point west of Salt Lake City and for all business originating in the East and going west of that place, the receipts to be divided equally. Russell gave bond in the amount of $100,-000 for the performance of the work by his company, which was signed by Benjamin Holladay.[196]

The Western Stage Company, through its president, E. S. Alford, contracted to discontinue all service west of Fort Kearny and to keep stages running between that place and Omaha. For this concession it was

195 Hafen, p. 211.
196 Contract between Russell and William B. Dinsmore, March 16, 1861.

paid $20,000 per year, 70 percent by the Central Overland California & Pike's Peak Express Company and 30 percent by the Overland Mail Company. This contract cleared the Central Route of all competition and gave those two companies a monopoly on all overland mail, passenger, and express business west of the Missouri River.[197] Russell viewed the prospect opened by the signing of these contracts and his optimism mounted. On March 20, 1861, he forwarded the contracts to Waddell.

. . . . believing them to be all the Co. could ask and as much as I ever encouraged them to hope for, and with all an A No. 1 contract, one that will pay big money if well managed, I am very content [he said]. We should get the thing up right, work it with energy, and with its results entirely relieve R. M. and W. I am detained preparing my public statement.

Presumably Russell went west within a fortnight after the delivery of the contracts to Waddell. His public statement had been widely circulated and read with interest. Naturally he was the most talked about man on the frontier. Old friends, who were more or less inclined to sympathize and view the bond matter through his eyes, flocked to welcome him. On April 26, in a meeting of the stockholders of the Central Overland California & Pike's Peak Express Company, he resigned as its president. This may have been understood when the contracts with the Overland Mail and Western Stage Companies were signed in New York. Bela M. Hughes, his old friend and agent at St. Joseph, was elected in his stead.[198]

Although Russell remained a director and stockholder in his express company, he was now without authority or responsibility in it. Both he and his associates clearly recognized the somber fact that his usefulness to the concern as an officer and financier was ended. If it was to be saved, an executive with an untarnished reputation was necessary.

One of the primary questions confronting the express company was where the mail line to Salt Lake City should run. At that time it followed the old emigrant route from the Missouri River to Fort Kearny. From there it went to that city by way of the Platte River, South Pass, and Fort Bridger, with a branch line running from Julesburg to Denver. This was an excellent route, but the rush of people to Colorado and the building

---

[197] Contract between Russell and E. S. Alford, March 16, 1861.
[198] *Kansas Historical Quarterly*, XIV, 78.

of towns and mining camps in the mountains created a demand for a more satisfactory mail service.[199] It was therefore proposed that a new route running through Denver and on to Salt Lake City be laid out.

The officers of both the Central Overland California & Pike's Peak Express Company and the Overland Mail Company being willing that this should be done, a line along the Cherokee Trail through Bridger's Pass and Fort Bridger was proposed. Early in April, John S. Jones made the people of Denver a proposition that, if they would build stage stations from that city to Fort Bridger and construct bridges on the North Platte and Green Rivers, the express company would accede to their wishes.[200] This was not quite what the people wanted. They insisted that the route should run west from Denver up Clear Creek and were certain that a pass in the mountains to the west could be found.

On May 6, 1861, Russell and Bela M. Hughes arrived in Denver for the purpose of choosing a route for the line. It had to be in operation by July 1 and there was no time to lose. This was Russell's first trip across the Plains and to Denver. The enthusiastic welcome accorded him must have warmed his heart after his experiences in Washington. Newspapers spoke of him in glowing terms, and in the latter part of the month a great ball was given in Golden in his honor. On this occasion he shared the spotlight with William Gilpin, first Territorial Governor of Colorado.[201]

In the meantime an exploring expedition, financed by Coloradoans and under command of Captain E. L. Berthoud, was assembled at Empire City. Its purpose was to find a pass over the mountains along the Clear Creek Route. On May 8, James Bridger arrived in Denver to help locate the stations along the line. They took to the mountains and on May 12 discovered the pass which today bears the name of the leader of the party.[202]

After spending some time making further explorations, blazing a trail on the east side of the range and examining the country on the west as far as the Colorado River, they returned to Golden, whence a message was sent to Russell at Denver. Taking a coach to Empire City, he examined the new route, belived it to be a good one, and spent a short

199 *Rocky Mountain News,* April 17, 1861. 202 *Ibid.*
200 *Kansas Historical Quarterly,* XIV, 77.
201 *Ibid.,* p. 78.

time at Idaho Springs. Here his passion for investment in budding enter-prises asserted itself. Before he left he had bought a number of town lots and mining claims.[203] He also, about this time, became interested in the development of the hot sulphur springs on the western slope and acquired four-sevenths of the land upon which they were situated.

After inspecting the new route, he returned to Denver, took a spe-cial coach, and hurried back to Leavenworth for orders, making a record trip of three days and twenty-one hours. Going to someone else for orders was something new in his experience. He laid the whole matter before the Board of Directors of the Express Company who decided to send Bridger and Berthoud out along the line to examine it, locate stations, and mark the road. The route they chose was west from Denver over Berthoud Pass to Hot Sulphur Springs, where it turned northwest to the headwaters of Yampa River, which it followed to near the mouth of Little Snake River. At this point it turned southwest to White River, and ran along it to Green River. Crossing that stream it went up the Uinta, crossed the Wasatch Mountains, struck Provo River, and followed it to the town of that name on Utah Lake. From there it ran to Salt Lake City.[204]

By the time the route had been determined upon, the first of July, the deadline for starting service on the Central Route, was at hand. Since the new road was not ready they had to start the coaches over the old one by way of South Pass.

The route over Berthoud Pass was never used. In July, 1862, the line was changed to the Cherokee Trail. It ran from Denver up the South Platte to the mouth of Cache la Poudre Creek, which it followed to Virginia Dale. Crossing the Black Hills and the Laramie Plains, it rounded Elk Mountain and struck the North Platte near the mouth of Sage Creek. Crossing that stream, it ran through Bridger's Pass, crossed the Red Desert, ran down Bitter Creek to Green River, then followed Black's Fork to Fort Bridger. Here it joined the old route.

Under the circumstances which existed in 1861, everyone connected with the Central Overland California & Pike's Peak Express Company felt that as good an arrangement as could be hoped for had been made. No one was discouraged with it, for as Russell said, the contract with

203 *Kansas Historical Quarterly*, XIV, 78.
204 Hafen, pp. 222, 223.

the Overland Mail Company was A No. 1, and would pay "big" if well managed and worked with energy. While the line was being gotten ready someone, probably Russell himself, got up a long "Estimate of Receipts and Disbursements" and sent it to Waddell. This old, yellowed document tells an eloquent story of human hopes and expectations. It also reveals much concerning the short history of the Central Overland California & Pike's Peak Express Company. It showed, among other things, that it would cost $476,642 to operate the line from the Missouri River to Salt Lake City from May 1, 1861 to July 1, 1862. During that time the receipts from passengers, Pony Express, and express business were estimated at $1,083,480. This allowed a net profit of $606,838. It was also shown that by July 1, 1864, the net profit on the venture, including $449,-758 worth of horses and mules on hand, would amount to $1,200,000.

Broken down into specific items, these estimates present valuable data upon the operation of the express company. Some of the more important items were:

DISBURSEMENTS MAY 1, 1861, TO JULY 1, 1862

45,000 bushels of corn . . . @ .50		$22,500.00
Hay for 50 stations . . . . @ $400.00		20,000.00
Rations 150 men 330 days		20,000.00
Quarterly forage & board from [Ft.] Kearny east .		36,000.00
Pay 250 drivers		81,250.00
5 Division agents		4,500.00
Extra agents		2,500.00
Transportation, grain 2,610,000 lbs, 300 rations, average 450 miles		63,542.00
Telegrams		2,500.00
Shops, repairs		7,500.00

In addition there were old debts and the $20,000 bonus to the Western Stage Company to be paid. Receipts were estimated as follows:

Mail pay	$ 476,000.00
Passengers	249,600.00
Express between Missouri River, Denver and Salt Lake City	104,000.00
Pony Express	100,000.00

Receipts from the Pony Express were based upon five hundred letters per trip after July 1, 1861, when reduced rates would go into effect. Whoever made the estimate remarked that those receipts would be greatly more than realized, as would the Denver and Salt Lake City passenger and express receipts. In addition, he said, the Express Company had a train of twenty-nine wagons which would save several thousand dollars on transportation. While plans were being made to put the line into operation, the Civil War exploded in their faces. Fort Sumter fell on April 14, and the Battle of Bull Run was fought three weeks after they got the line into operation. With the beginning of this titanic struggle, the interest of the nation was no longer focused upon the development of the West.

By the time the express company was ready to begin operations under the new arrangement, it owed Benjamin Holladay $200,000, on account of his having endorsed and accepted drafts from time to time since the contract with the Overland Mail Company was made. On July 5, 1861, at a special meeting of the Board of Directors, five of the seven being in attendance, President Bela M. Hughes was unanimously authorized to execute a note and deed of trust upon the company and all its property in favor of Holladay. For some reason, possibly to avoid publicity, this was not carried through until about four and a half months later. On the following November 22, Hughes and John W. Russell, secretary, gave Holladay a bond of $400,000 and a mortgage upon the company, which was to run three years. In the meantime Holladay would continue to honor drafts, bills of exchange, acceptances, and advance money as required on condition that the total for the past and future should not exceed $300,000. On the same day the company made a deed of trust to T. F. Warner, Holladay's old partner, and Robert L. Pease, an employee, as trustees, naming Holladay as the beneficiary.[205]

This strategy also proved hopeless. Less than three weeks later, Holladay declared Russell's bond of $100,000 forfeit and requested the trustees to sell the company. On December 6, 1861, they advertised that it would be sold at auction to the highest bidder at the Massaiot House in Leavenworth on the 31st of the same month. Other creditors secured an injunc-

[205] *Federal Cases,* Book 21, p. 307. Mortgage, The Central Overland California & Pike's Peak Express Company to Benjamin Holladay, Nov. 22, 1861. J. V. Frederick, *Ben Holladay: The Stagecoach King,* pp. 1, 40, 65.

tion against this sale, and the company went ahead as usual. Heroic efforts were made to put it upon a paying basis but without success. So dire were the straits into which it had fallen that its employees derisively dubbed it "Clean Out of Cash and Poor Pay." At length the injunction was dissolved, and on February 15, 1862, it was again advertised for sale on the following March 7. There was no interference this time, and Holladay bid it in for $100,000. He said it owed him $208,000.[206]

Two of the directors of the company, Webster M. Samuel and Alexander W. Street, made an issue of the affair. On April 1, 1862, they requested their fellow officials to begin legal proceedings to have the sale of the company set aside. When this was refused, they brought suit themselves, alleging that the sale was illegal. They won their case in the United States Circuit Court, Kansas Territory, which found that it was without authority and in violation of trust.[207]

The matter did not end here. In October, 1869, the same court heard another suit brought by Samuel and rendered the same decision. Both cases were dismissed when the United States Marshal could find no one representing the company in his district upon whom to serve a summons.[208]

The failure of Russell, Majors & Waddell and the Central Overland California & Pike's Peak Company was a catastrophe of nation-wide proportions. When news of it was broadcast, the host of creditors took whatever steps they thought best in an effort to protect their interests. There was not much they could do, for the assets and resources of the principals were already in the hands of trustees.

One class of creditors, those holding Secretary Floyd's acceptances, had been almost entirely omitted from the deeds of trust made by Russell, Majors & Waddell. This was probably because everyone concerned with the acceptances expected that they would be liquidated with funds accruing from pay for transportation. Among these were Pierce & Bacon, of Boston, Mass., who held $260,000 worth. On November 12, 1861, they wrote Floyd's successor, Simon Cameron, asking that they be paid. Nothing whatever was done about it. They wrote him again on February 4, 1862, with no better results. Some six weeks later, on March 18, Edwin

206 Hafen, *op. cit.*, p. 227. Frederick, *op. cit.*, p. 282.
207 James McCahon, *Reports of Cases,* etc., pp. 214, 229.
208 *Federal Cases,* Book 21, p. 310.

M. Stanton having succeeded Cameron, they wrote again. This time they enclosed an opinion of Charles B. Goodrich, a Boston attorney, concerning the legality of the acceptances and a copy of the statement of John Perry Sellar showing that the total amount of that paper outstanding was $861,000. It was Goodrich's opinion that they were legal and should be paid.[209]

Pressure upon the War Department caused Secretary Stanton to lay the whole matter before Attorney General Edward Bates on April 21 with a request for an opinion as to their legality. This was given under date of July 20. He contradicted Goodrich's opinion and declared that the acceptances were not legal because Secretary Floyd had no authority to accept or endorse them.[210]

Meanwhile various holders of them had appealed to Congress for relief. Among them was the Bank of the State of Missouri, the Franklin Savings Association of St. Louis, and Pierce & Bacon. These appeals were in the form of memorials which were referred to the Committee on Judiciary. On July 16, Senate Bill No. 102 for their relief was reported.[211] After considerable debate this was defeated. No further attempt to gain relief through Congressional action was made by anyone.

On July 8, 1862, House Bill No. 554 to reimburse the Indian Trust Fund for the abstracted bonds was received in the Senate and referred to the Committee on Indian Affairs. It was passed and signed by President Lincoln on the 15th. The total cost to the United States, including $50,-066.64 for interest, was $710,458.65,[212] not a dollar of which was recovered from the firm of Russell, Majors & Waddell or the estates of the partners. Nor were any of the bonds, which had passed into the hands of innocent purchasers, recovered.

When the question of relieving those who held Secretary Floyd's acceptances was before Congress, it was suggested the matter be laid before the Court of Claims. Attorney General Bates remarked in his opinion that it seemed rather strange and suspicious that this had not been done, for there both the equity and law relating to them could be heard and determined. On June 17, 1862, Benjamin E. Bates of Boston, through

---

[209] *H.R.,* 36th Cong., 2d sess., Report 78, pp. 302-10. Goodrich, *Opinion,* pp. 13, 16.

[210] Edward Bates, *Opinion,* etc., p. 16.

[211] *U.S. Congressional Globe,* 37th Cong., 2d sess., p. 3401.

[212] *U.S. Congressional Globe,* 37th Cong., 2d sess., p. 202; Appendix, p. 397. Greenberg to the author, Dec. 18, 1937.

Charles B. Goodrich, presented to the Court a claim for $15,000, the face value of acceptances he held. The case was extended to the October term, 1863, when it was declared that the United States was not obligated to pay him because Secretary Floyd had no authority to issue them.[213]

Having failed in obtaining relief from Congress, T. W. Pierce, representing Pierce & Bacon, the Dover Five Cent Saving Bank, E. D. Morgan, and the Boatmen's Saving Institution of St. Louis also sought redress in the Court of Claims. That Court ruled as it had in the Bates case. Pierce then appealed to the United States Supreme Court, where the case lay until the December term, 1868. The opinion handed down, six of the Justices concurring, was that the judgment of the Court of Claims should be affirmed. The others dissented upon the ground that Secretary Floyd had authority to issue the acceptances. The illegality of them being thus established, there was nothing for the unfortunate investors to do except absorb their losses as best they could or look to the trustees of Russell, Majors, and Waddell for payment.[214]

213 *Bates* vs. *The United States,* Court of Claims, Case No. 1889.
214 U.S. Supreme Court, Opinion, 7 Wall., 666.

XV

AFTERMATH

WITH THE SALE of the Central Overland California & Pike's Peak Express Company to Holladay, Russell passed from the scene as freighter, merchant, stage coach proprietor, and mail contractor. Other men, building upon the foundations he and his partners laid, reaped the rich harvest they deserved to garner. His visit to the Rocky Mountain region early in the summer of 1861 aroused a feverish, though belated interest in the affairs of that new frontier. Now his incurably sanguine temperament stood him in good stead. He cheerfully wrote off his losses, locked in his heart whatever pain he may have felt over the turn affairs had taken, and resolutely set to work to repair his wrecked fortunes. Although bankrupt and under a cloud, he was, at forty-six years of age, the same virile, magnetic Russell he had always been.

Circumstances favored his effort to stage a financial come-back. Nobody in Colorado appeared to discount him because of what had happened in Washington. Old friends sympathized with him and new ones did not care anything about it. His name still carried weight and partners for whatever he wished to undertake could easily be found. The country was filled with men like himself who were willing to take chances, even long ones. The pattern of things here was similar to that in Lafayette County and Lexington when he had become a clerk in Aull's store thirty-two years before. The mines had proved their worth, new discoveries were constantly being reported, commerce was established, and agriculture had passed the experimental stage. Nobody was better qualified by disposition and experience to sense the opportunities in these things than he.

Being already interested financially in the town of Idaho Springs and the vicinity, he set to work promoting the area now embraced in Clear Creek County. When it appeared that the Central Overland California & Pike's Peak Express Company stage line might run through Denver and over Berthoud Pass, his enthusiasm flamed as of old. Naturally the

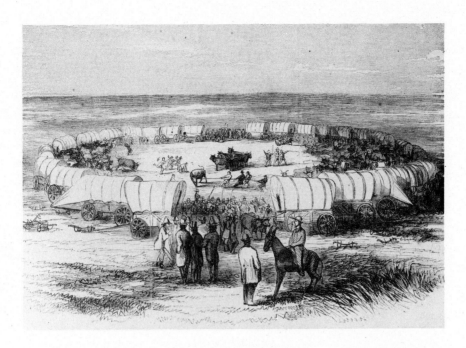

Government Trains on the Route to Utah
From *Frank Leslie's Illustrated Newspaper*, January 8, 1859
(*Courtesy of the Nebraska State Historical Society*)

Pacific Railroad bulked largely in his dreams. He, as well as everyone else, expected it to follow the stage line. When it did, Idaho Springs would become an important health and recreation center. Believing that he stood upon the threshold of a fabulous new era, he organized the Colorado and Pacific Wagon, Telegraph, and Railroad Company in midsummer, 1861. The first Colorado legislature incorporated it that fall.[215] It was intended that the wagon road should run west from Denver, through Idaho Springs, and over Berthoud Pass. When the railroad was built it would follow the same route.

Russell and his associates were not alone in their hopes and expectations. Everybody in Colorado shared them to the full. "Open this wagon road," declared the *Rocky Mountain News,* May 27, 1861, "and the telegraph and railroad will follow as sure as sun rises and sets." When Congress passed the Pacific Railroad Bill in July, 1862, this newspaper voiced satisfaction with it. "Denver will yet be the great halfway station between New York and San Francisco," it prophesied. Unfortunately it did not happen that way. When the Clear Creek route was surveyed by competent engineers the incline was found to be too steep for a railroad and the whole proposition suffered an eclipse.[216]

While still hopeful concerning the outlook for this concern, Russell organized the Clear Creek and Hot Sulphur Springs Wagon Road Company, which was incorporated by the Colorado Legislature August 18, 1862. Meanwhile, probably following the failure of the first wagon road venture, he went back East and became cashier of the Kansas Valley Bank at Atchison, Kansas, of which Waddell was then president.[217] Work on this road began in 1862 and carried on until December, when the weather forced a halt until spring. Capital did not flow in as expected, but work was resumed in the spring of 1863. This scheme suffered the same fate as the other in that the road did not reach Berthoud Pass. That ended Russell's effort at road building and railroading.

While promoting his wagon roads he was also laying the foundation for what he hoped would be a fortune in mining claims and water and mill rights in the Clear Creek, Dailey, Banner, and Grass Valley districts. His partners in this business were William E. Sisty, H. D. Sherwood,

215 *Colorado Magazine,* IX, 164.
216 Hafen, *op. cit.,* pp. 229, 230.
217 Kansas Valley Bank Note, No. 13680.

John Armor, and Samuel A. Walsh. He also helped organize and promote the New York Gold Mining Company, some of whose stock was sold by Webster M. Samuel. In company with Sisty, Armor, William L. Campbell, Lafayette Beebe, and Charles C. Bangs, he organized the Hot Sulphur Springs Town Company, four-sevenths of the stock being assigned to himself.[218]

None of his mining claims proved to be bonanzas, although in 1863 it was reported that his mine on the Silver Mountain Lode near Empire City was producing between two and three thousand dollars' worth of gold per week. Early in 1865 he was back in New York. With Thomas P. Akers and a man by the name of Pease, he opened a brokerage office at 17 New Street under the title of Akers, Russell & Pease. Their chief business was speculation in gold and dealing in Colorado mining stocks. Now, as always, he found people willing to lend him money, but only in relatively small amounts. Gone were the days when his name upon a note or draft was worth hundreds of thousands of dollars. His splendid residence at 686 Broadway was sold, his family remained in Missouri, and he was housed in a second-rate boarding house. He still maintained an office at 111 Broadway but his residence was at 176 Fifth Avenue. The Brevoort House, which he once boasted of inhabiting, and Delmonico's knew him no more.[219]

By April 1, 1865, his affairs were so complicated again that they were unmanageable. On that date he went through the familiar process of assigning his property to trustees for the benefit of creditors. This time they were James P. Rogers and his second son Charles Benjamin. He listed the Johnson County, Missouri, lands mentioned in his deed of trust to Eugene B. Allen and Elbridge Burden, January 30, 1861, and his interest in mining properties in Colorado.[220]

On May 14, 1866, he made another deed to his son John W. which was subject to that of the year before. The greater portion of his indebtedness was for loans from individuals in small amounts. He owed his son John W. $22,500, his son Charles Benjamin $2,992, and Webster M. Samuel $600 for groceries and interest. Included also were some of the debts listed in his deeds of trust in 1861. Total liabilities under this deed

[218] Russell, Deed of trust to John W. Russell, May 14, 1866.

[219] *Rocky Mountain News*, Apr. 7, 1863. Russell, Petition by debtor, Apr. 3, 1868, Schedule A No. 3. Trow. *New York City Directory*, 1865-66, p. 841. Russell to Waddell, Aug. 24, 1859.

[220] Russell, Deed of trust to James P. Rogers and Charles B. Russell, Apr. 1, 1865.

of trust were $136,903.43.[221] The catalogue of loans in this document emphasizes the straits into which he had fallen. His very name, once a synonym for financial power, was either forgotten or spoken with derision. Now he was experiencing what he himself foresaw five and a half years earlier when he remarked that "the censorious world would attach moral guilt" in the event of failure.

When he had borrowed all the money he could from relatives and what friends remained to him, he was through. Then there was nothing left for him except long memories and the crushing weight of debt upon his conscience. On February 28, 1868, he wrote a pathetic letter to his old partner Waddell.

Some months since, your son John wrote me relating to the bankruptcy law, which I replied with the best light before me. Since which I have learned that (with management) we can do it and be fully relieved from the Gov't, as well as individuals, and I would go ahead if I had the money. My attorneys will prosecute it for me and take their pay after I get through and when I can conveniently do so. But the incidental expenses here and to arrange at Washington so that we will meet no opposition from the Interior Department who hold Floyd's accept. $870,000.00, will require 4 to $500. Now if you are disposed to pay one half of that or say $200 send me that sum and so soon as I complete and have my list of liabilities printed will furnish you a copy, from which alone I think you can ever get up a perfect list of R. M. and W's liabilities, especially as there are many that in the future would give you trouble of which I presume you know nothing. Again I can serve you in the Interior Dep't. That is the most important item of all. If I had the money I would go ahead and you could have the benefit without contributing a cent, but I have it not, and how to raise the other 2 or $300 I scarcely know. Yet I will do so in some way. I am at work perfecting my list of liabilities preparatory to making application. . . .

Whether Waddell sent the sum requested or not, Russell completed his application for a decree of bankruptcy and filed it in the District Court of the United States for the Southern District of New York on April 3, 1868.[222] Under Schedule A-No. 1, preferred creditors who were to be paid in full were listed. The only one recorded was the United States government to which was due the sum of $870,000, the value of the abstracted bonds.

[221] Russell, Deed of trust to John W. Russell, May 14, 1866. Russell to Waddell, June 19, 1860.

[222] Russell, Petition by debtor, April 3, 1866.

Schedule A-No. 2 contained the names of creditors holding security for loans amounting to $606,121.12. Among these were banks and individuals who held Secretary Floyd's acceptances and the notes of Russell, Majors & Waddell and the Central Overland California & Pike's Peak Express Company.

Creditors whose claims were unsecured for $631,020.61 were listed under Schedule A-No. 3. The name of Alexander Majors headed this list. There was due him an unnamed amount on account of a debt of Russell & Waddell to Russell, Majors & Waddell and $24,851.66 because of a debt by Miller, Russell & Company to the same firm. Among others to whom debts were acknowledged under this schedule were Jerome B. Simpson $60,629.84, James N. Simpson $10,000, Eugene B. Allen and Alexander Street $115,898.78 under a note given by Benjamin Holladay and Russell in 1858 to Russell, Majors & Waddell and endorsed by them, and Benjamin Holladay $14,609 for cash and notes endorsed and paid by him. Also included under this schedule were debts of $150 for room rent and $596 for office rent.

Schedule A-No. 4 showed liabilities on notes or bills discounted which should have been paid by the drawers or acceptors. These included $290,-000 worth of Secretary Floyd's acceptances. The total liabilities listed in all the schedules amounted to $2,498,630.85. According to this petition, Russell, Majors & Waddell owed in 1860, including $870,000 for the abstracted bonds, the sum of $1,662,342.16. When debts incurred by Russell after that date, which were not chargeable to the freighting firm, are deducted the previous figure for its indebtedness at that time is seen to be approximately correct.

Waddell was in a better position to weather the storm of adversity than either of his partners. While making his assignments in 1861 he executed a deed of trust to his spacious home on South Street to his son John W. for the sum of one dollar and an agreement to pay a certain debt of $8,000.[223] By this arrangement he was privileged to live on serenely in the midst of familiar surroundings. He never engaged in business of any kind again, unless it was in a small way or as an extremely silent partner.

The Civil War raged around him for four years, the Battle of Lexington was fought almost on his doorstep between General Sterling Price

[223] *Record Book* J, No. 1, Lafayette County, Mo.

and Colonel James A. Mulligan, September 18-20, 1861, one of his sons was killed protecting a slave, his home was raided again and again, and he was compelled to sign an oath of allegiance to the United States. On September 27, 1868, John W., with his brothers and sisters, made a deed of trust for the family home to James G. Byram as trustee for their mother, Mrs. W. B. Waddell.[224]

Although Waddell had signed his property over to others in one way or another, he was not freed from harassments of various kinds. Lawsuit after lawsuit was filed against him; land he owned was sold on the courthouse steps for taxes; and angry, disappointed creditors vilified his name and attacked his honor and integrity. Loss of fortune, tragedies accompanying the Civil War, grief over the harsh attitude of former friends and business associates, and inactivity bore heavily upon him. By the time he reached his late fifties he was broken in spirit and health.[225]

One of the concerns which had always lain close to his heart was the Baptist Female College. He had given generously of his time and money to it and was anxious about its welfare. It, too, had suffered from the ravages of war. In 1862 Federal troops occupied its building, and academic work ceased for about five years. When the Board of Trustees again took up the task of promoting it, the first problem was to find a suitable place to carry on its work. Since the building in Old Town had been all but wrecked by Federal troops, it was believed that a new one was desirable. This problem was solved on October 27, 1869, when James G. Byram, trustee for Mrs. Waddell, deeded the Waddell home to the college for $11,500.[226]

Waddell's autumn days were spent at the farm home of his daughter, Mrs. A. G. Williams near Lexington. He died on Sunday, April 1, 1872, and was buried in Machpelah Cemetery, not far from his old home, which he helped to found many years before. The college, to which he gave freely and to which his handsome residence was sold, outlived him forty-four years and closed its doors in 1916. The old building which housed the office of Russell, Majors & Waddell at the northwest corner of the public square in Lexington suddenly collapsed many years ago.

William Bradford Waddell, like his partners, Alexander Majors and

[224] Minutes, Board of Trustees, Lexington Baptist Female College, Aug. 13, 1869.

[225] Alonzo Slayback to Waddell, Oct. 25, 1866. Waddell obituary, *Lexington Caucasian*, April 13, 1872.

[226] Minutes, Board of Trustees, Lexington Baptist Female College, Aug. 13, 1869.

William H. Russell, was truly a remarkable man. As a frontier business entrepreneur he had no superior west of the Mississippi River. His years spanned the period in which the frontier leaped the Great American Desert and firmly planted itself upon the golden sands of the Pacific Ocean. His genius was that of the small town merchant, banker, and financier. Left to himself, he probably would never have been anything more. Without William H. Russell, unshadowed prosperity would undoubtedly have attended him all the days of his life. Unfortunately he fell under Russell's irresistible influence, shared his grandiose dreams, and sacrificed all in a hopeless effort to transmute them into reality. To his grief he discovered, when it was too late, that he had hitched his wagon, not to a fixed, reliable star, but to a brilliant earth-bound meteor.

Out in New York, Russell faded day by day. Financiers who had formerly listened respectfully when he spoke were now too busy to even see him. His schemes, and he had them, no longer interested anybody. He quickly became a stranger in Wall Street and there was small occasion for maintaining contacts with bankers. With the passing of the months the obscurity which was inexorably enfolding him deepened. Now he turned to about the only means of earning a livelihood left to him, selling a patent medicine called "Tic Sano," an "antidote" for neuralgia.[227] In addition he advertised that he was a notary public and Commissioner for all the States and Territories. In due time his health began to fail. This could have been expected, for no man of his temperament and disposition could live under the conditions now surrounding him.

About the time of Waddell's death, which must have cast a deep shadow over his heart, his son, Charles Benjamin, and son-in-law, Webster M. Samuel, went to New York and took him to the home of the latter in St. Louis. After a brief time there he was moved again to the home of his son, John W., who was a banker at Palmyra, Mo. Here he died on September 10, 1872.[228] He was buried in the cemetery at that place and to this day no stone with his name upon it marks his resting place. The town newspaper honored his passing with scarcely a quarter of an inch of space and that of his home town, Lexington, did not mention it at all.

Sic transit gloria mundi!

[227] *Rocky Mountain News,* June 7, 1872.

[228] *Dictionary of American Biography,* XVI, 252. Mrs. W. J. Boyer, Sketch of William H. Russell, MS.

SELECTED BIBLIOGRAPHY

F<small>OR THE SAKE OF BREVITY</small>, well-known sources of general information concerning Russell, Majors & Waddell, the freighting and stagecoach business, the Pony Express, and the general history of the period covered in this book have been omitted. Care has been taken, however, to include all new, original, and previously unused source material.

Act to Incorporate the Central Overland California & Pike's Peak Express Company. Pamphlet. Waddell Collection, Huntington Library.

A<small>KERS</small>, T<small>HOMAS</small> P. Letter to William B. Waddell, Dec. 26, 1860. MS, Waddell Collection, Huntington Library.

A<small>LEXANDER</small>, C<small>OLONEL</small> E. B. Letter to Colonel S. Cooper, Oct. 9, 1857. U.S. H.R., 35th Cong., 1st Sess., Ex. Doc. 2, pp. 29-30.

A<small>NDREAS</small>, A. T. *History of Kansas.* Chicago, 1883.

A<small>ULL</small>, J<small>AMES</small>, and A<small>ULL</small>, R<small>OBERT</small>. "Letter Books," II, III, IV, and V. MSS, Lexington (Missouri) Historical Society.

———. "Order Book," V. MS. Lexington Historical Society.

———. "Receipt Book," V. MS. Lexington Historical Society.

B<small>ANGS</small>, A. O. Letters to William B. Waddell, Feb. 9 (2), 10, 1859. MS, Waddell Collection, Huntington Library.

B<small>ANCROFT</small>, H<small>UBERT</small> H<small>OWE</small>. *History of Oregon.* 2 vols. San Francisco, 1886.

———. *History of Utah.* San Francisco, 1890.

B<small>ANNING</small>, C<small>APTAIN</small> W<small>ILLIAM</small>, and B<small>ANNING</small>, G<small>EORGE</small> H<small>UGH</small>. *Six Horses.* New York, 1928.

B<small>ARTLESON</small>, J<small>OHN</small>. "Diary," December 1 to 20, 1857. H.R., 35th Cong., 1st Sess., Ex. Doc. 2, pp. 52-56.

Bates, Benjamin E. vs. the United States. U.S. Court of Claims. Gen. Juris., Case No. 1889. National Archives, Washington, D.C.

B<small>ATES</small>, E<small>DWARD</small>. *Opinion . . . on the Validity of Acceptances Given by John B. Floyd to Russell, Majors & Waddell Now Held by Pierce & Bacon.* National Archives, Washington, D.C.

B<small>ECKNELL</small>, C<small>APTAIN</small> W<small>ILLIAM</small>. "Journal of Two Expeditions from Boon's Lick to Santa Fe." *Missouri Historical Society Collections,* Vol. II.

———. "Journal of Captain William Becknell." *Missouri Historical Review,* Vol. IV.

B<small>ERTHOLD</small>, V<small>ICTOR</small> M. "William H. Russell, Originator and Developer of the Famous Pony Express." *Collector's Club Philatelist,* Vol. VII.

Book of Original Entries. Lafayette County, Missouri.

BOYER, MRS. W. J. "Sketch of William H. Russell." MS. Loaned by Mrs. John W. Russell.

BRADFORD, ROBERT B. Letters to William B. Waddell, Mar. 31, Apr. 30, Sept. 13, 22, Oct. 13, 19, Nov. 3, 21, 29, Dec. 8, 15, 22, 1859; Jan. 5, 12, 18, 25, 26, Feb. 2, 3, 23, Mar. 8, 15, May 1, 3, 9, 14, 16, June 5, 14, 19, July 4, 6, 18, 20, Aug. 13, 25, Nov. 9, Dec. 8, 10, 21, 1860; Jan. 8, Feb. 1, 1861. MSS, Waddell Collection, Huntington Library.

———. Petition to Supreme Court, First Judicial District, Colorado, Sept. 28, 1861. MS, Waddell Collection, Huntington Library.

BRADLEY, GLENN D. *The Story of the Pony Express.* Chicago, 1913.

BROWN, ALBERT G. Warrants for the arrest of Joseph Taylor and William Stowell. H.R., 35th Cong., 1st Sess., Ex. Doc. 71, pp. 55, 56, 68.

BYERS, CHARLES. Letters to William B. Waddell, Jan. 6, Dec. 24, 1858; Feb. 4, 1859. MSS, Waddell Collection, Huntington Library.

CASE, THEO. S. *History of Kansas City.* 1888.

Central Overland California & Pike's Peak Express Co. *Dr.* to R. B. Bradford & Co., 1860. MS, Waddell Collection, Huntington Library.

CHAPMAN, ARTHUR. *The Pony Express.* New York, 1932.

CLARK, CAPTAIN H. F. Letter to General A. S. Johnston, Nov. 4, 1857. H.R., 35th Cong., 1st Sess., Ex. Doc. 71, pp. 62-63.

Colorado Magazine, Vols. VII and IX.

Contract between William H. Russell, Alexander Majors, and William B. Waddell, Dec. 28, 1854. (Photograph in library of the author.)

Contract between William H. Russell, Alexander Majors, and William B. Waddell, Dec. 18, 1856. MS, Waddell Collection, Huntington Library.

Contract of Majors & Russell with Captain Thomas L. Brent, Feb. 16 ,1857. Records of the War Department, Quartermaster General, Consolidated File, National Archives, Washington, D.C. Also in *A Brief Statement of Claim.* Waddell Collection, Huntington Library.

Contract between Russell, Majors & Waddell and Captain Thomas L. Brent, Feb. 16, 1857. Records of the War Department, Quartermaster General. Consolidated File, National Archives, Washington, D.C.

Contract between Russell, Majors & Waddell and General Thomas S. Jesup, Jan. 16, 1858. Waddell Collection, Huntington Library. Also, Records of the War Department, Quartermaster General. Consolidated File. National Archives, Washington, D.C.

Contract between Russell, Majors & Waddell and subcontractors, Mar. 30, 1858. MS, Waddell Collection, Huntington Library.

Contract between William H. Russell, Alexander Majors, William B. Waddell, and Robert B. Bradford. MS, Waddell Collection, Huntington Library.

Contract between Russell, Majors & Waddell and John S. Jones, *et al.,* Oct. 28, 1859. MS, Waddell Collection, Huntington Library.

SELECTED BIBLIOGRAPHY

Contract between Citizens of St. Josephs, Missouri, and William H. Russell and William B. Waddell, representing the Central Overland California & Pike's Peak Express Co., Mar. 2, 1860. *Record Book,* X, Buchanan County, Missouri, 508-511.

Contract between William H. Russell, representing the Central Overland California & Pike's Peak Express Co., and William B. Dinsmore, representing the Overland Mail Co., Mar. 16, 1861. MS, Waddell Collection, Huntington Library.

Contract between William H. Russell, representing the Central Overland California & Pike's Peak Express Co., and E. S. Alford, representing the Western Stage Co., Mar. 16, 1861. MS, Waddell Collection, Huntington Library.

Contract between Russell, Majors & Waddell and Captain Stewart Van Vliet, Apr. 11, 1860. Records of the War Department, Quartermaster General. Consolidated File, National Archives, Washington, D.C.

Cooper, Jackson. Letter to William B. Waddell, Jan. 6, 1860. MS, Waddell Collection, Huntington Library.

Dictionary of American Biography. New York, 1933. Vol. XVI, p. 252.

Donaldson, J. M. Letter to the author, Aug. 23, 1945.

Estimate of Receipts and Disbursements. MS, Waddell Collection, Huntington Library.

Federal Cases, Comprising Cases Argued and Determined in Circuit and District Courts of the United States. Book 21. St. Paul, 1896.

Floyd, John B. Letter to James L. Orr, Apr. 6, 1858. H.R., 35th Cong., 2d Sess., Ex. Doc. 2, pp. 69-71.

Frederick, J. V. *Ben Holladay: The Stagecoach King.* Glendale, Calif., 1940.

Gates, Paul W. "A Fragment of Kansas Land History." *Kansas Historical Quarterly,* Vol. VI.

Gove, Captain Jesse A. *The Utah Expedition.* Concord, New Hampshire, 1928.

Goodrich, Charles B. *Opinion upon the Legal and Equitable Rights of a Bona Fide Holder for Value of Sundry Drafts Made by Army Contractors upon, and Accepted by, the Secretary of the War Department.* Washington, 1862. (Harvard University Library.)

Greenberg, Joseph. Letter to the author, Dec. 18, 1937.

Guckert, —. Telegrams to John W. Russell, July 16, 17, 1860. Waddell Collection, Huntington Library.

Hafen, Leroy. *The Overland Mail.* Cleveland, 1926.

Harlow, Alvin F. *Old Waybills.* New York, 1934.

Hays, W. S. Letters to William B. Waddell, Oct. 25, Dec. 4, 1860; Feb. 6, 1861. MSS.

Hawthorne, Hildegarde. *Oxteam Miracle.* New York, 1942.

Hinckley, C. S. Letter to William B. Waddell, July 10, 1860. MS, Waddell Collection, Huntington Library.

History of Clay and Platte Counties, Mo. St. Louis, 1885.

HORTON, JAMES C. "Personal Narrative." *Kansas Historical Collections,* Vol. X.

JOHNSTON, GENERAL A. S. Letter to Major Irwin McDowell, Oct. 13, 1857. H.R., 35th Cong., 1st Sess., Ex. Doc. 2, pp. 34-35.

JONES, RUSSELL & Co. Balance sheet, Nov. 1858. MS, Waddell Collection, Huntington Library.

Kansas Historical Collections, Vols. X and XI.

Kansas Historical Quarterly, Vols. I, VI, XI, XIII, and XIV.

Kansas City Directory, 1860-61.

Kansas Valley Bank Note, No. 13680. (Photograph courtesy Mrs. W. B. Waddell.)

LARIMER, GENERAL WILLIAM, and LARIMER, WILLIAM H. H. *Reminiscences.* Lancaster, Pa., 1918.

Laws of Missouri, 1854-55.

Lexington Baptist Female College, Minutes of Board of Trustees. (First Baptist Church, Lexington, Missouri.)

MCCAHON, JAMES. *Reports of Cases Determined in the Supreme Court of Kansas.* Chicago, 1870.

MAJORS, ALEXANDER. *Seventy Years on the Frontier.* New York, 1893.

——. Deed to William H. Russell and William B. Waddell, Mar. 20, 1857. MS, Waddell Collection, Huntington Library.

——. Deeds of trust to Alexander Street, Oct. 19, 1860; Feb. 25, 1861; to Alexander Street, Finis B. Ewing, and Eugene B. Allen, Feb. 26, 1861. *Record Book* 37, Jackson County, Missouri.

——. Letters to William B. Waddell, Mar. 11, 28, Dec. 9, 1858. MSS, Waddell Collection, Huntington Library.

MAJORS & RUSSELL. *Statement of the Claim of Majors & Russell for Transportation in 1857.* Pamphlet, 1857. Waddell Collection, Huntington Library.

——. *A Brief Statement of the Claim of Majors & Russell, also the Evidence upon Which It Rests.* Pamphlet, 1860. Waddell Collection, Huntington Library.

——. *Account of Losses Sustained in 1857.* Waddell Collection, Huntington Library.

Marriage Record No. 1, Jackson County, Missouri.

Marriage Record Book B, Lafayette County, Missouri.

Marriage Record, Vergennes, Vermont, 1816.

MARTIN, GEORGE W. "A Chapter from the Archives." *Kansas Historical Collections,* Vol. XII.

MILLER, A. B. Letters to William B. Waddell, March 1, Sept. 6, Dec. 3, 1858. MS, Waddell Collection, Huntington Library.

Minutes, Criminal Court, District of Columbia, 1861. Records, U.S. District Courts. National Archives, Washington, D.C.

SELECTED BIBLIOGRAPHY

MOREHEAD, CHARLES R., JR. "Personal Recollections," in William E. Connelley, *Doniphan's Expedition.* Kansas City, 1907. Pp. 600-620.

———. Family Record. Los Angeles (n.d.).

Mortgage given by the Central Overland California & Pike's Peak Express Co. to Benjamin Holladay, Nov. 22, 1861. *Record Book* 29, Buchanan County, Missouri.

Nebraska State Historical Society, *Publications, XX.*

Newspapers: *Kansas City Star, Lawrence Republican* (Kans.), *Leavenworth Herald* (Kan.), *Lexington Advertiser* (Mo.), *Lexington American Citizen, Lexington Caucasian, Lexington Weekly Express, Liberty Tribune* (Mo.), *New York Tribune, St. Joseph Weekly West* (Mo.), *Rocky Mountain News* (Denver), *St. Louis Era, St. Louis Reveille, St. Louis Tri-Weekly Republican.*

Petition of James N. Simpson vs. William H. Russell, *et al.,* Mar. 7, 1860. Box 61, Circuit Court, Lafayette County, Missouri.

PERRINE, FRED S. "Military Escorts on the Santa Fe Trail." *New Mexico Historical Review,* Vol. III.

Private Laws of Kansas Territory, 1859.

Record Books F, G, H, I, J, K, L, and M. Lafayette County, Missouri.

Records, Veterans Administration, War of 1812. Bounty Land File of Oliver Bangs, Warrant No. 7848.

Records, U.S. Court of Claims. General Jurisdiction, Case No. 1889. National Archives, Washington, D.C.

Record, U.S. District Courts. District of Columbia, Mar. 1861, Criminal Trials No. 33.

Record, District Court. District of Columbia, Criminal Sci. Fa. No. 1, Mar. 7, 1868.

RHODES, JAMES FORD. *History of the United States.* New York, 1895.

RISLEY, D. R. Estimate of wages due employees on road, May 30, 1859. MS, Waddell Collection, Huntington Library.

ROOT, FRANK A., and CONNELLEY, WILLIAM E. *The Overland Stage to California.* Topeka, 1901.

ROOT, GEORGE A., and HICKMAN, RUSSELL K. "The Pike's Peak Express Companies." *Kansas Historical Quarterly,* Vols. XIII, XIV.

RUSSELL, WILLIAM H. Deeds of trust. To James N. Simpson, Dec. 31, 1860; to Eugene B. Allen, Jan. 30, 1861; *Record Book* J, No. 1, Lafayette County, Missouri. To James P. Rogers and Charles B. Russell, Apr. 1, 1865; *Record Book* L, Clear Creek County, Colorado. To John W. Russell, May 14, 1866; *Record Book* Q, No. 1, Lafayette County, Missouri.

———. Statement to Select Committee, Jan. 16, 1861. H.R., 36th Cong., 2d Sess., Report of Committee No. 78, 333-38.

———. "Statement to the Public," *St. Louis Tri-Weekly Republican,* Apr. 4, 1861; also, *Rocky Mountain News,* Apr. 7, 1861.

Russell, William H. Petition by debtor, Apr. 3, 1868. *Records, U.S. District Courts*. Southern District of New York, Bankruptcy Case No. 1290. National Archives, Washington, D.C.

——. Letter (n.d.). MS.

——. Letters to William B. Waddell, Feb. 27, Mar. 20, 26, 31, Apr. 13 (2), 16, 24, 29, Oct. 24, 25, 1858; Feb. 27, Mar. 6, Apr. 12, 14, 17, 24, 29, May 5, Aug. 19, 22, 24, 30, Nov. 22, 28, Dec. 30, 1859; Jan. 3, Mar. 20, May 1, 11, 12, June 9, 13, 14, 15, 19, 22 (2), 29, 30, July 8, 10, Aug. 5, 13, 15, Oct. 11, 19, Dec. 16, 19, 21, 1860; Dec. 11, Apr. 12, 1861; Feb. 7, 1868. MSS, Waddell Collection, Huntington Library.

——. Letter to Samuel & Allen, Sept. 29, 1860. MS, Waddell Collection, Huntington Library.

——. Telegram to William B. Waddell, John S. Jones, and Alexander Majors, July 6, 1860. MS, Waddell Collection, Huntington Library.

——. Telegram to William B. Waddell and Executive Committee, July 12, 1860. MS, Waddell Collection, Huntington Library.

Russell, Mrs. J. W., "Russell Family History." MS.

Russell, Majors & Waddell. "Instructions to Wagon-Masters." Leaflet. Waddell Collection, Huntington Library.

——. Letters. To John B. Floyd, Jan. 8, 1858; to J. B. Simpson, Oct. 31, 1860. MSS, Waddell Collection, Huntington Library.

——. "Rules and Regulations for the Government of Outfits," Pamphlet. Waddell Collection, Huntington Library.

——. Statement of Assets (n.d.). MS, Waddell Collection, Huntington Library.

——. Statement of bills due from Dec. 1859 to Aug. 1860. MS, Waddell Collection, Huntington Library.

——. *Train Books*. Loaned by Louisa P. Johnson.

Sage, Rufus. *Out of the West*. New York, 1913.

Scudder, John. "The Pony Express," *Lexington Weekly Express,* Aug. 22, 1888.

Slayback, Mrs. Alonzo. "Genealogy of the John Waddell Family." MS. Loaned by Mrs. J. W. Russell.

Slayback, Alonzo. Letter to William B. Waddell, Oct. 25, 1866. MS, Waddell Collection, Huntington Library.

Smoot, L. R. Letter to William B. Waddell, MS, Dec. 18, 1858. Waddell Collection, Huntington Library.

Trow. *New York City Directory,* 1865-66.

U.S. Congressional Globe. 37th Cong., 2d Sess.

U.S. H.R. 34th Cong., 1st Sess., Ex. Doc. 17.

——. 36th Cong., 2d Sess., Report of Committee, 78.

——. 31st Cong., 2d Sess., Ex. Doc. 1.

SELECTED BIBLIOGRAPHY

U.S. H.R. 32d Cong., 1st Sess., Ex. Doc. 1.

——. 36th Cong., 2d Sess., Report of Committee on Military Affairs.

U.S. Sen. 31st Cong., 1st Sess., Ex. Doc. 1, p. 295.

——. 31st Cong., 1st Sess., Ex. Doc. 26, p. 24.

——. 31st Cong., 2d Sess., Ex. Doc. 11, p. 15.

——. 32d Cong., 1st Sess., Ex. Doc. 1, p. 295.

——. 33d Cong., 2d Sess., Ex. Doc. 68.

——. 36th Cong., 2d Sess., Report of Committee on Military Affairs.

U.S. Supreme Court. Opinion. 7 Wall. 666.

WADDELL, JOHN W. Letters to William B. Waddell, Mar. 11, 27, 30, Apr. 2, 3, 5, 13, 21, May 1, Nov. 8, Nov. 25, 1858. MS, Waddell Collection, Huntington Library.

WADDELL, WILLIAM B. Letters. To W. S. Hays, Jan. 22, 25, 1861; to John W. Waddell, Mar. 27, 1858. MSS, Waddell Collection, Huntington Library.

——. Deeds of trust. To John W. Waddell, Jan. 23, 1861; to Elbridge Burden and John W. Waddell, Jan. 30, 1861; to John W. Waddell and Elbridge Burden, Feb. 1, 1861. *Record Book* J, No. 1, Lafayette County, Missouri.

WADDELL, WILLIAM B., Obituary of. *Lexington Caucasian,* Apr. 10, 1872.

Waddell financial statement (n.d.), MS, Waddell Collection, Huntington Library.

Waddell & Russell. Kansas lands account. MS, Waddell Collection, Huntington Library.

War Department, in account with Russell, Majors & Waddell (n.d.), MS, Waddell Collection, Huntington Library.

Warder family history. MS. Loaned by Mrs. R. G. Champion.

WORNALL, FRANK. Statement to the author, 1940.

WELLMAN, PAUL I. "The Silent Partner." *Kansas City Star,* Nov. 22, 1942.

WELLS, DANIEL H. Letter to Joseph Taylor, Oct. 4, 1857. H.R., 35th Cong., 1st Sess., Ex. Doc. 71, pp. 57-62.

WYMAN, WALKER D. "The Military Phase of Freighting on the Santa Fe Trail." *Kansas Historical Quarterly,* Vol. I.

YOUNG, WILLIAM. *History of Lafayette County, Missouri.* Indianapolis, 1910.

YOUNG, BRIGHAM. "Proclamation," Sept. 5, 1857. H.R., 35th Cong., 1st Sess., Ex. Doc. 2, pp. 32-33.

INDEX

A

Abstracted bonds: cause trouble, 55; story of, 95-107; not refunded by Russell, Majors & Waddell, 130; refunded by the United States Government, 130

Acceptances: agreement of Secretary Floyd to endorse, 24, 100; protested, 59, 96, 97; past due, 95, 96; $300,000 worth about to mature, 98; written October, 1860, 101; outstanding, 115; holders demand payment by Secretary of War, 129; legality of, 130; holders appeal to Congress, 130

Akers, Thomas P., Attorney for William H. Russell, 111, 113

Akers, Russell & Pease, speculators in gold, 134

Alexander, Colonel E. B., 17, 19, 20

Alford, E. S., President Western Stage Company, 92

Allen, Eugene B., assignee, 55

Allen, James S., partner of William H. Russell, 6

Allen, Russell & Company, 6

Alta Telegraph Company, 82

Annual Post Route Bill, 1861, 121

Army of Utah, x, 17, 18, 20, 21, 22, 62

Armor, John, 46

Aull, James, 5, 6

Aull, Robert, frontier chain-store operator, 5; interest in freighting, 7, 8

B

Babbit, Almond W., mail carrier, 70

Bailey, Godard: a poor man, 96; gives Russell $150,000 worth of bonds, 97; an embezzler, 98; learns Russell, Majors & Waddell still financially embarrassed, 99; delivers $387,000 worth of bonds to Russell, 100; delivers $333,000 worth of bonds to Russell, 103; receives $870,000 worth of acceptances from Russell, 103; letter to Secretary Thompson, 103; calls upon Senator H. M. Rice, 103; gives acceptances and receipt to Senator Rice, 104; note to Wagner, 104; warrant issued for arrest, 105; before Cabinet, 105; did not appear before Select Committee, 110; arraigned, 110; case against dimissed, 100

Baltimore & Ohio Railroad, viii

Bancroft, H. H., 113

Bangs, Lieutenant Oliver, 5

Bank of America, 24, 58

Bank of Republic, 24, 59

Baptist Female College, and Civil War, 137

Barrett, R. W., 19

Bartleson, John T., 18

Bates, Attorney General Edward, on legality of acceptances, 130

Bear River, 20

Becknell, Captain Wm., 1, 2

Beni (Reni), Jules, trading post established by, 46; killed by Slade, 46

Benton, Senator Thomas Hart, "Father of the West," 66; appropriation from Congress, 66; favored transcontinental railroad, 66

Berthoud, Captain E. L., leader of exploring expedition, 135

Berthoud Pass, 126, 132, 133

Big Sandy Creek, 19

Black's Fork, 19, 20, 22

Black, Jeremiah S., Secretary of State, 104

Blanchard, W. L., mail contract of 1852, 73

Bond scandal, 95-107

Bradford, Catherine, wife of John Waddell, 9

Bradford, R. B.: signs bond, 4; wrote Waddell, 26; criticizes Leavenworth & Pike's Peak Express Company, 45; system of orders, 45; forms partnership, 50; view of conditions, 50; business activities, 51; built toll road, 51; organizes fire insurance company, 51; buys ranch, 52; organized Capital Hydraulic Ditch Company, 52; road paying well, 52; represents Russell, Majors & Waddell, 52; urges Russell, Majors & Waddell to buy various concerns, 52; criticized, 53; controversy with Waddell, 53; to Leavenworth and Lexington, 54; sues Russell, Majors & Waddell, 56; gives up office of Leavenworth & Pike's Peak Express Company in Denver, 78; builds Central Overland California & Pike's Peak Express Company stations, 78

Bradford, R. B. & Company store in Denver, 50; building, 50; importance of, 50; supplies to Central Overland California & Pike's Peak Express Company, 54; sold to Russell, Majors & Waddell, 54; dissolved, 54; accounts against and credits for Central Overland California & Pike's Peak Express Company, 78

Bradford Road, 51, 52

Bradley, Glen D., statement concerning Pony Express, 74

Brent, Captain Thomas L., 17, 23

Bridger, James, guide, 20; helped locate stations, 125

Bromley, James E., division agent, 44; buys horses, 75; Salt Lake City agent Central Overland California & Pike's Peak Express Company, 78

Brown, James, 3, 4, 7; partner William H. Russell, 4; partner John S. Jones, 7; Brown, Russell & Company, 7

147

Nebraska City in Overland Freighting Days
From Majors' *Seventy Years on the Frontier*
(*Courtesy of the Nebraska State Historical Society*)

Leavenworth in 1858
(*Courtesy of the Leavenworth Public Library*)

INDEX

Fields, Henry, 51
Fields, Martin, postmaster of Denver, 41
Filligrew, messenger, 47
Finney, William W., San Francisco agent of Central Overland California & Pike's Express Company, 78; puts line into operation, 79
Flour, for Utah troops, 48; contract criticized, 49
Floyd, John B., Secretary of War, 74, 112, 113; acceptances, 24; asked to produce contracts, 25; refuses resignation, 34; agrees to flour contract, 49; endangered by acceptances, 96; wife of Bailey related to, 96; resigns as Secretary of War, 105; relation to bond transaction, 105; case against dismissed, 106; returns to Washington, 106; indicted by District of Columbia grand jury, 106; moved to Virginia, 106; suspected by Select Committee, 109; before Select Committee, 109
Fontenelle Creek, 20
Fox, Dr. John M., general agent at Denver, 40; office in Denver, 41
Freighting monopoly, 11, 34, 58
Frey, Johnny, said to be first rider to leave St. Joseph, 82
Fort Bridger, 21, 22, 23, 26, 71
Fort Leavenworth base of supplies, 3; assembly point Army of Utah, 17; recruits to, 23

G

Gilbert & Gerrish, 48
Gilpin, William, promoter of Centropolis, 66; first territorial governor of Colorado, 125
Goodrich, Charles B., 130
Greeley, Horace, editor *New York Tribune,* 42; in Utah, 49
Green River, 19
Gwin, Senator W. M., 74, 76, 90, 91

H

Hamilton, Wm., first Pony Express rider to leave Sacramento, 83
Ham's Fork, 19, 20
Hannibal & St. Joseph Railroad, 81
Hanks, Ephraim K., mail carrier, 71
Harney, General S. W., 17, 20
Hays, Wm. S., agent for Russell, Majors & Waddell, 55; instructions to, 55
Heywood, Bishop Joseph L., postmaster of Salt Lake City, 70
Higgins, Alfred, mail carrier, 71
Hinckley Express Company, 92, 93
Hobbs, Dr. J., agent for Russell, Majors & Waddell, 58
Hockaday, J. M. & Company, sold contract to Leavenworth & Pike's Peak Express Company, 43; provisions of contract, 43; fees on line, 47; mail contract, 1858, 72
Holladay, Benjamin: forms partnership with Russell, 48; in Utah, 49; trustee, 107
House Bill No. 554, to reimburse Indian Trust Fund, 130

House of Representatives: calls for contracts, 34; favorable report on Whitney plan, 66; resolution authorizing Select Committee to ask certain questions, 112
Hughes, Bela M., president Central Overland California & Pike's Peak Express Company, 124

I

Indian Trust Fund, 98, 99
Irwin, Richard B., 115

J

Jefferson City, Mo., railroad to, 66
Jersey wagon, vii
Jesup, Quartermaster General Thomas S., 18, 24; notice for transportation, 48
Johnston, A. S., 20, 21
Jones & Russell, 8, 117; store in Denver, 46, 47
Jones, Russell & Company, 50, 52; store, 46, 51; advertise for horses, 79
Jones, Charles O., 7
Jones, J. B., agent for Central Overland California & Pike's Peak Express Company, 54; to Denver, 61; Denver agent for Leavenworth & Pike's Peak Express Company, 78
Jones, John S.: organizes Leavenworth & Pike's Peak Express Company, xiii; signs bond, 4; partner of James Brown, 7; general manager, Leavenworth & Pike's Peak Express Company, 35; proposes stage company, 35; wagon trains to gold diggings, 35; putting line into operation, 38; getting stages off, 40; route superintendent, 45; shareholder Central Overland California & Pike's Peak Express Company, 57

K

Kansas City starting point, 63
Kansas land bought by Russell, Majors & Waddell,
Kearney, General, S. W., 3
Kimball, Hiram, contract, 1856, 72
Kilgore, Wilson & Company, 24

L

Landis, Israel, Pony Express saddles made by, 80
Larimer, General William, calls on Russell, 33; plans Town Company, 34
Larimer, William H. H., 33; assistant postmaster at Denver, 41
Lathem, Robert W.: testimony, 105; meets Russell in New York, 106; worked for Floyd, 109; before Select Committee, 109; difficult witness, 109
Lea, Luke, 96; before Select Committee, 108
Leavenworth Fire and Marine Insurance Company, 16
Leavenworth, Kansas: headquarters for Majors and Russell, 14; news of gold, 33; celebrates return of stagecoaches, 41
Leavenworth, Pawnee & Western Railroad, 16

INDEX

SUTTER'S FORT • CAMP FLOYD • FORT MORGAN • FORT KEARNEY • FORT MACKAY • FORT LEAVENWORTH • FORT BUSS.

O R E G O N

I D A H O

SIMPSON'S TRAIN BURNED

SUBLE

DAWSON & BARRETT TRAINS BURNED

Fort Winfield

Ft-Bridger

Great Salt Lake

ROU

Camp Sc

Carson City

C A L I F O R N I A

P O N Y   E X P R E S S

Salt Lake City

N E V A D A

SACRAMENTO

Camp Floyd

U T A H

PROPOSED C·O·C & P
(UNUSED)

Fort Wingat

A R I Z O N A

N

Fort Yuma

BUTTERFIELD OVERLAND MAIL ROUTE & EMIGRAN
TRAIL TO CALIFORNIA

EMPIRE

• SANTA FE TRAIL •